I Almost Blew Out The Light

A MEMOIR

KAREN CONNOR

PLATYPUS
PUBLISHING

Est. 2014

ISBN 978-1-965016-52-7

To my friends who always encourage me

and who accept me as I am

To my family who love me and put up with me

To all those who have been bullied, to those who are being bullied and for everyone who knows someone being bullied

You inspire me to write and keep me going

Acknowledgments

To my husband Kevin and my sweet babes, Emily and Noah; thank-you for standing beside me, thank you for putting up with my hyperactivity and everything that comes along with it and thank-you for loving me anyway. You are my world, my life. You are loved more than you will ever know.

To Bobbi Boudreau; thanks for taking my idea for the cover of this book and making it a reality, for being my long-time best friend and for always being there for me no matter what. I love you!

To Andrew Lawlor, my editor, my friend; Thankyou for your patience and thoroughness going through my book. Thank-you for making it reader ready. You have made a dream of mine come true.

To Matt Rudd and the Platypus Publishing team; Thank-you for teaching me so many new things and for supporting and encouraging me along the way.

Contents

Preface

If I had given up, if I had gone through with it, I wouldn't be here to tell you my story, to share my experience. I would have been quickly forgotten; a candle blown out too soon, why, because no one knew. I kept it all to myself, lying to my family that everything was fine.

If I did blow out the light, what purpose would that have served? None. No one would have learned anything, no one would have known why. Just another tragedy where no one knew the reason. People would have said, "She showed no signs, there were no warnings". I wonder what kids at school would have said. Did they hear anything? Did they see anything? Did they know something was wrong? If asked, what would they have said?

Some who are struggling are transparent with those around them, while many choose to keep their challenges to themselves. Everyone's reasons are different, I can tell you why I chose to stay silent.

I felt ashamed. I felt guilty. I felt I deserved it.

In addition, I didn't want people to think I was a loser, or to feel sorry for me. I felt that if I admitted it was all real, then I would have to start reliving, explaining, justifying... I thought it would be too much and that I would go overboard. In the end, I decided it would be better to pretend everything was ok, than to admit I was barely surviving.

Looking back, I wish I had told someone. Not just anyone, though, an adult: my school counsellor, my parents... any adult that I could trust and that could have possibly helped me survive better than I was on my own. I am writing this, 30+ years later, sobbing and hyperventilating - scared of reliving it, scared of dealing with all the feelings I have repressed for decades. I guess that's why it took me so long to work up the courage to write this book.

Well, here goes...

Chapter 1

In The Beginning

I grew up in Fredericton, on the Northside of town in a little place called Nashwaaksis. I came from a decent middle-class family. My dad was a respected member of the fire department; my mom, like a lot of moms at that time, did not work while my sister and I were young. A lot of moms stayed at home, taking care of the house and being there when their kids got home from school.

Fredericton is a small city of about 80,000 residents. It is the capital of New Brunswick and is on the East Coast of Canada. Both my parents grew up in or near Fredericton. My mother was one of seven siblings, and my dad has one brother. Their siblings stayed in Fredericton and most started their families there too, so naturally my parents decided to raise their family there as well. They were also Northsiders, my dad grew up in Devon and my mom grew up in Nashwaaksis.

These towns were about a 10-minute drive from each other. Between Devon and Nashwaaksis lies Fredericton's Wolastoquey Indigenous Nations Community.

Fredericton is a pretty city with lots of trees, there is a river that runs between the North and South sides of town. There are 4 seasons here, winter, spring, summer and fall. My favorite times of year are summer and fall because of the warm temperatures and the beautiful changes in the color of leaves in the fall. The leaves change from various shades of green to yellows, oranges and reds. In my opinion, the red colors are mesmerizing with the brightest reds coming from the leaves of sugar maple trees. Red is my favourite color so that may be the reason I think red fall leaves are the most beautiful.

The downtown area of the Southside is the main business district. There are a lot of local restaurants, government workers and local businesses in that area, including police, a theatre and an art museum. Two universities lie on the hill just a few minutes' drive from the downtown core. Main Street is the street that mostly runs by the river on the Northside. There are a few chain restaurants, car dealerships and other businesses along there. The majority of the rest of the area near the river are personal dwellings.

The wide river that separates the north and south sides is the heartbeat of the city. If you looked skyward down, the river would be the heartbeat, the streets the veins and all veins connect to, and lead to, the heart.

There are lots of beautiful geese and different kinds of ducks that call the river home between spring and early winter, there are several islands in the river marking untouched natural growth, and eagles line the borders of the majestic white pines along the riverbanks. In the warmer months you can see people fishing, canoeing, kayaking, rowing and boating on the river and people walking or running along both sides of the river on either the paved walkway on the southside or the crushed rock trail on the northside. There are also several feet of mowed green spaces on both sides of the river where people have picnics or just rest, enjoying the beautiful scenery. There are a couple of parks on the southside with lots of trails to enjoy as well.

About 25 minutes from the city centre is a beach and a couple of campgrounds for residents and tourists. The campground and park are vast and even contains a small golf course.

While my hometown was idyllic, that wasn't always the description for me. I was a handful, right from the start. I had (and still have) Attention-Deficit/Hyperactivity Disorder (ADHD) a condition where someone has trouble focusing, staying still, and controlling their impulses, often leading to behaviors like fidgeting, talking excessively, interrupting others, and acting without thinking, making it hard to manage daily tasks at school or work; essentially, it's a pattern of difficulty paying attention and managing activity levels that can affect different areas of life. These are, of course some of the disadvantages of ADHD – but there are advantages. One advantage is that I can quickly forget why I was mad at something. I can get over little things quickly, with the emphasis on 'little things'. It also means that I annoy quickly – at least that's how I see it - others might say I am quick to anger. I also had trouble focusing in school, which meant I had to work harder than most, just to get half-decent marks.

The hyperactivity part of ADHD meant I was hyper as a child, quickly excitable and full of energy. I loved to climb, and not just trees. Rooftops, garages and the refrigerator in my home were all climbing gyms for me. I loved gymnastics – tumbling, cartwheels, handsprings and swinging on the bars.

I liked to make people laugh, and felt I was fun-loving and carefree. Not everyone saw me that way, though. Some people simply found me too much (probably more than just 'some'), and some felt compelled to call me "weird". I remember the times when it happened and how confused I was. I kept thinking "I know who the weird kids are", and I didn't think I was one of them. It really threw me off, I wasn't seeing what they were seeing. In fairness, I think I

3

just made them uncomfortable. They likely didn't know how to take me or couldn't handle my excess energy. I guess we have to put labels on the things we can't understand... seems fair, right?

I thought I had a great childhood, at least for a while. I was from a good family and there were always tons of kids around my neighbourhood - we ruled the local outdoor pool. I was athletic and, even though my parents kept my hair short, I was a decentlooking kid.

We also had the best sledding hill on our property. In the winter, all the neighborhood kids would come to my house, ring the doorbell and ask if my sister or I wanted to slide with them so they could slide there too. A lot of kids were a few years older, and we were known by them because of our hill. Even at elementary school, older kids knew my name and would say hi in the hallways and on the playground at lunch. Because of all of that, I felt special, I had some confidence. Other kids in my classes would ask me how I knew all these older kids, both English and French. It may have made them jealous, but it made me feel cool.

I had a large extended family. My mother was one of seven children, and since most of us lived in the same city we always had family around. We would have these big family Christmas potlucks, and they only got bigger as the 'children' started having their own children. It should have been great, but I only had two cousins close to my age and the older ones saw us as immature and annoying at the time.

On the north side of Fredericton, there was a divide between English kids and the kids in French Immersion. If you were to put us in general categories, I guess the French Immersion kids generally came from families with a bit more money, parents who may have had better jobs, more ambition, etc. The Englishonly kids seemed to be the opposite, tougher somehow. These are

4

generalizations, I know there were English-only kids who were small, with happy, successful parents. Either way, most kids stayed with 'their own kind'.

That stuck me right in the middle. I knew a lot of kids from both sides, and if I was seen to be favouring one group or the other, they would call me out on it. The English kids liked me because I wasn't stuck up like they felt the rest of the French Immersion kids were. I could never understand why we couldn't all be friends. I didn't want to be seen as stuck up, so I only had a couple of close French Immersion friends at a time, and they tended to be more like the English kids. In the end, it led me to feel like I didn't fit in anywhere.

Knowing a lot of kids, especially older ones, did give me a bit of an attitude. I felt pretty cool; and I felt if I got in trouble, there would always be someone who had my back. My experiences at that time made me dislike girls I considered mean, or who thought they were better than everyone else. I thought they needed a taste of their own medicine. If I was told someone was a bitch, I believed it - and so had an instant dislike for them. It was unfair of me; I know that now. At the time I had neither the experience, nor the attention-span to understand the consequences of my actions. I would say something, shooting from the hip, which would prompt dirty looks, or an insult exchange. For me, that was it, I usually forgot about it and moved on. I never stopped to think I might actually be hurting someone's feelings. Bitches don't have feelings, right? Think back, did you ever make another kid feel bad? How do you feel about it now?

Chapter 2

A Bit About Me

My name is Karen. I have a small build, long brown curly hair and hazel eyes. When I was young, I had a spunky attitude, wasn't scared of anything, and didn't take shit from other kids.

Back then there were a lot of kids in my neighborhood and if you were in the house and told your parents you were bored, they'd tell you to go outside and find someone to play with. There was no fear of something bad happening, it was like there was a collective, blind ignorance, a thought that nothing bad would happen.

My parents struggled with me because of the ADHD. I climbed walls, trees, even fridges (as mentioned). I was in constant motion, legs going a mile a minute – which is still true to this day. I wasn't a bad kid, I just needed help to reign it in. Looking back, I feel for my teachers in elementary school – they just didn't have the tools to deal with kids like me. Most thought that I was a troublemaker, or stupid, or just bad. That stings to this day. I wish they had known I had no ill intent, that I didn't realize I was so disruptive in class and that I was actually pretty smart. Only two of my elementary school teachers knew better, they made me want to learn, and I behaved well in their classes (most of the time...).

I had a best friend in Grade 1. We were attached at the hip and the bad thing about that is, it led me to be disruptive in class. Why? Well one on particular day all the kids were sitting at their desks, probably working on writing or simple math. My best friend asked me to come over and talk to her. I made a gesture signifying not right now but she was adamant, so with no awareness of the fact that I may be disruptive to the other kids or disrespectful to my teacher, I simply got out of my chair and went to her seat a few rows back and started a conversation with her, right in the middle of class. I don't even remember what she wanted... something about what we were going to do at lunchtime. Well, we weren't doing anything at lunchtime because I got in trouble and the teacher kept me in at lunch. I blamed my friend instead of taking responsibility. I remember feeling like she made me do it, like I had to do it because she asked me to. And I was fuming that the teacher felt I was being rude. That was not my intention at all, I just didn't realize the effect my actions were having on the class.

Being that I didn't have a lot of actual friends, and that I liked to make the friends I had laugh, I choose a few guys to 'bully'. Not the capital B bully but enough. There was this one guy, he... well, he had a head shaped like a peanut. That is a bit of an exaggeration, but that's what I thought at the time. I also thought it would be funny to run by, push his head forward with my hand and yell, DOHHHIIINNNNG. It wasn't malicious, at least in my mind, and it did result in me getting the laughs. He wasn't laughing though. I guess my desire to make people laugh made me unaware of how he might feel, again not an excuse... just reality in living with ADHD. I enjoyed being a jokester, I thought it made people like me. I also thought it would be hilarious to walk behind someone, lift their leg with my foot and push it to their other leg super-fast. What resulted is a triplike motion that never caused them to fall, just kind of trip. People laughed, thought it was funny and I knew I wasn't physically hurting anyone...I didn't think about mental pain though. To this day, I don't think anyone was too bothered by my 'sense of humor', they probably just thought I was an asshole.

Chapter 3

Shirts Off Everyone

My mother used to get calls from my elementary school almost every day. "Your daughter did this, your daughter did that..." Can you imagine what that must have been like for her? Looking back, I imagine she must have dreaded the phone ringing during school hours. Like the collection calls for bills you just can't pay. One day she had enough and told the school,

"You take care of her at school, I'll take care of her at home". And that was that. ADHD symptoms have been reported throughout history, but it wasn't really recognized as a disorder until the 1980's, and it certainly wasn't talked about like it is today. I think some of my teachers were just frustrated and didn't know what to do with me, maybe they were looking for guidance thinking my mom knew what to do. Well, she didn't either.

I was labeled by most faculty in the school as a 'bad' kid. At the beginning of a school year, my new teacher would often say, "Oh, I've heard about you" or something close to that. Obviously, they had been warned by my previous teacher. It was tough to feel, as a child, judged before they ever laid eyes on me. I'm not sure that would feel good at any age. Mom had to 'deal' with me at home, a lot of the teachers thought I was bad news, and I haven't even mentioned the rest of my family.

I was puzzled by things I thought were unfair, like "boys can do that, but girls can't". I am a matter-of-fact kind of person, and if I think something is dumb or doesn't make sense, then I will probably challenge it. It was the end of grade 2 when summer weather arrived early in Fredericton, and there was no air conditioning in my school. You were lucky if you were sitting by the window, getting the tiniest breeze. The boys in the class asked if they could take their shirts off. The teacher said yes, so I figured I was allowed too. Man did that ever kick up a shit storm. I hadn't gotten my shirt off the whole way before the teacher was hollering at me to put it back on, saying I wasn't allowed to do that. I was livid – we were seven years old – all our chests looked the same. I was so innocent, I never thought what I was doing had a negative perception in society. I grew up with a sister and no brothers, so I guess conversations on the difference between girls' and boys' bodies never came up. And I wouldn't let it go. I expected an answer that made sense and of course, there was none. I even had some of the other girls and boys agreeing with me. In the end, I'm sure you know what happened. The girls had to keep their shirts on, and I was, once again, labelled the troublemaker. I was left confused; I just couldn't understand why boys and girls were treated differently and I wanted to know why.

For the first time, I was made to feel ashamed of my body, that showing it is inappropriate. Speaking about shame, shame on that teacher for doing that to me. I know she was coming from what she thought was a good place, but she turned something so innocent into something dirty, something bad. After a bit more arguing, I put my shirt back on fully. I think she even got the principal to come down. Well, there's another X in my file.

Shortly after that incident, the teacher I had in first grade accosted me in the hallway. Paraphrasing, she asked something like "Who do you think you are?" and "What makes you so special?". I eventually realised that the 'shirt-off' incident must have been discussed in the staff room, but I still didn't get why she was so mad at me. Having someone in authority say that to me really threw me off, especially since I still didn't see what was so wrong with what I had done. It made me wonder if I really was a bad kid.

I was hauled into the office the next day, which was a rare occurrence in elementary school. I was scared. The principal's office was behind the open area where all the administration women worked, facing the playground at the back of the school. I don't remember the principal's name, but I do remember he was in his late fifties or early sixties, and he had a huge, long desk (of course everything looked big to a kid). He sat behind that huge desk, waiting for me to come in. I can't recall exactly what he said, but it was something about me thinking I could do whatever I wanted. Again, I was dumbfounded. Later it occurred to me it was probably my former teacher who had taken the issue to the principal. For some reason, she had an axe to grind with me, and felt I needed to be taught a lesson. I remember thinking that any other kid would have probably just been given a warning – but at this point they had had enough, and that was not to be the fate of this "bad kid". I was getting 'the strap'.

For those unfamiliar with 'the strap', it's corporal punishment consisting of a leather belt struck across your butt. I couldn't believe I was getting the strap. Was I that bad? I was a good kid, albeit a misunderstood one. I went to church, I believed in God, I loved my family, and I believed that most people were good. Does questioning a believed hypocrisy constitute beating a child with a leather belt? No. Not then. Not ever.

I protested, to no avail. He told me to take my pants down and lay across his knees. WTF? So, in order to teach me to not take off my shirt, they made me pull down my pants and lay across the lap of a stranger? He removed the belt from his pants, loop by loop, and I felt so weird but didn't feel like I could defy him or tell him this was wrong. Reluctantly, I obeyed. Thank God, he let me keep my panties on.

He struck me with his belt. I laughed. I often laughed out of context as a child, especially when nervous, confused or overwhelmed. I even laughed while attending my first ever funeral. It was so quiet, which made me nervous, then I just couldn't sit still. I just couldn't help myself.

The principal struck me with his belt for a second time. This time, I cried. I thought doing it twice was unfair, which made me cry. That stupid fuck, I hope he laid awake all-night thinking about what he had done. He gave in to someone else's ideal of how bad kids should be disciplined. It may have bothered him, because I never heard of anyone ever getting the strap again.

Anyway, that was fun….

Chapter 4
A New Friend?

As I said, this was an age when parents sent you outside if you said you were bored. Well, I took this as a call to adventure and started walking around the streets near my house.

My neighborhood was middle-class – nice homes, nice families, lots of trees. My street looped around like a horseshoe and there were lots of side streets too. There were kids everywhere, not a lot were my age, though. Most were either my sister's age or older, otherwise they were younger than me.

I was an adventurous kid. I liked to explore places; I wondered what people's houses looked like on the inside and I had a great imagination. Every big house I saw, I wondered if it had a secret passageway and thought how cool that would be. One day, on one of my adventures, I was about halfway around the corner of my street, and I still hadn't found anyone I really wanted to get to know so I was going to turn back. Being the adventurous person I was, I decided to skip through someone's yard without much regard for it being someone else's property. I thought it was cool to see if I could sneak through unseen.

I approached the driveway of a pale yellow two-storey home, there was a car in the driveway, but all was quiet. Beside the garage was a nice, big pine tree – I wanted to climb that tree and jump on the roof of the garage, but I refrained. All seemed good until a yellow lab came running at me, barking it's head off. Man, that dog scared the shit out of me. Thankfully, I was fast and managed to get out of range before the dog got me, it got hauled back with a yelp as the dog reached the end of its chain. As I ran around the back of the garage I ran right into some girl.

She was very petite, with long, white-blond hair down to her ass, and her eyes were green. We were both startled and not sure what to say. I found out she lived at the house I was cutting through, and that we were only a year apart. Her name was Gwen.

After a short conversation I decided to head home but before I could go, Gwen asked me for a piece of gum. I told her the only one I had was in my mouth. She still wanted some though, but I said no. Then she asked to see my hand, top side up. I thought what in the hell does she want to see my hand for, but I showed it to her anyway. That little bitch took my hand and bit it really hard, then she took off running so I ran after her, I wanted to pummel her. I was pretty fast and would have caught her, but I stopped at the entrance to her house. With the screen door wipe-open and me about to come in, I saw Gwen with who I assumed was her mother at the bottom of the stairs in a room in the basement.

Turned out the lady was her stepmother, though I don't think her dad and the lady were married. She held Gwen hard by the arm asking what the heck was going on. Gwen wouldn't tell her what she did, but her mother-in-law knew by the anger on my face that Gwen had done something to upset me. Gwen's mother-in-law seemed to get angrier and angrier, and I turned to go because I was starting to get scared, but her mother-inlaw told me to stay put, so I did. Finally, the mother-in-law gave up on Gwen telling her and asked me. I didn't want to tell her, but I did after a bit of coaxing. I cried as I told her and showed her the teeth marks on my swollen, red hand.

The mother-in-law said she would hold Gwen and told me to come down and bite Gwen back, but I didn't want to. Then she did something I never would have suspected her to do. She took Gwen's hand and told her she should know what it feels like, so she bit Gwen. I don't know how hard, but Gwen was screaming and crying. Man, I couldn't stand it anymore, I ran home as hard and as fast as I could and thought those people are nuts and I don't want to see them again.

Would you believe that Gwen and I became the best of friends for the next 5 years? Weird how the oddest of situations can bring people together.

Chapter 5

The Old Car

Gwen and I spent almost every day together. I was an early riser and so was she so one or the other would arrive at each other's doorstep as early as 7:00 am.

There was an interesting place near Gwen's house. A small baseball field with trees all around the edges. Being the curious type that I was, I wondered what was in the woods beyond the trees. I was a bit weary of getting lost, but my curiosity got the better of me.

I convinced Gwen to check it out with me and promised we would not go further then where we can still see how to get back. It's always darker and cooler in the woods where the trees are large and the canopies are full, it also creates an ambiance of secrets and dread but maybe that was just all the horror movies I watched.

Big trees leave big spaces on the ground between each tree, making it easier to walk, unless there were roots sticking out. It was beautiful back there and I felt so free just exploring with my best friend, no one knowing where we were or what we were doing. I can understand how that would make some fearful - what if something happened to them? It wasn't seen as smart to go into the woods alone. For me though, the thought of being alone made me feel powerful, I felt alive.

While we were exploring, I spotted a car that looked like it was in an accident with dirt and grass growing on the hood and around the sides. The front of the hood was deeply dented, and it looked like it had been there for a very long time. It was definitely an antique; you could tell by the way the hood was curved at the edges. I think the car was mauve, but it may have looked that way because of the rust.

I was so excited. I had never been that close to a car that wasn't mine or one that I wasn't a passenger in. Gwen stayed back a bit, but I couldn't help myself, I had to check it out. All kinds of ideas were swimming in my head. Was there a car accident, did anyone know about it, did the people in the car die?

I told Gwen we should check for ID and wondered what we might find - a wallet, some money or something even crazier like a weapon. At the time, I had no idea what drugs were, otherwise that would have entered my mind as well. I can't explain the excitement I felt, it was like being half-scared of what we might find and at the same time I couldn't leave without going into the car and feeling between the seats, opening the glove box, seeing if we could open the trunk.

I decided to touch the car, to move my hand along the door frame and finally I went inside. The seats still had decent cushioning but were certainly aged with time. I checked everywhere but never found anything except for a broken pen and lots of dirt and rocks. Still, I was pretty proud of myself for checking it all over.

When we decided to head back out, a man living in the house that backed onto the woods asked us what we were doing. He seemed almost mad – it could have been his property, but I think he was more worried about us stealing something from his yard. I was so annoyed; we were two little girls aged 7 and 8 and we were just having a good time. He was totally killing my vibe. Anyway, I told him what we had seen, and he said there used to be a racetrack back there in the day and it was dented because of a smash up with another race car.

Not as cool as what I had thought but close. I still don't understand why someone would abandon their car to haunt the woods though.

Chapter 6

The Prairies

Another place Gwen and I discovered is what we called "the prairies". It is actually in the same area as the woods and the baseball field, at the end of a dirt road. The edges of the road were covered with shrubs, tall grass, and trees. In the summer there were ducks swimming in ponds adjoining the road and, in the winter, you could find a few people skating on the ice, even though it wasn't very smooth.

The prairies were a special place for me and Gwen. It was like our secret spot and no one else seemed to know about it. When we reached the end of the dirt road the rest of the world melted away and a new world came to life. It was literally like one minute you were in the dark and gloomy woods and the next step you took you were in a world of light; it was like you just cross an invisible barrier to another world. This world was vast, open and bright.

I can't speak for Gwen, but I felt so free out there, the adrenaline that I felt was amazing. We could run just for fun, explore as much as we wanted and for as long as we wanted. No one knew we were there which could be a bad thing I suppose but I didn't care, I loved being there too much to allow there to be any fear. Being there was like being in Peter Pan's Never Never Land, if only I could fly. Well, we sure could pretend though. When we ran, we would pretend that we were fairies, like Tinkerbell, beautiful, sparkly, and we had fairy dust that helped us fly. We imagined finding treasure that would be ours and ours alone. It was totally possible too, you never know what you might find when you just go out somewhere and look around and I don't think anyone else went out there, at least we never saw anyone when we were out there.

I named it the prairies because it reminded me of the long, tall grass that separated Anne and Diana's houses in Anne of Green Gables. Whenever Anne was out heading to Diana's or to anywhere else, the movie always showed her walking through a vast open area of tall grass and that's what our special area reminded me of, so we called it the prairies.

It was dreary and dark along that road to the prairies, even in the summer. Once you reached the end, though, everything was wide open, and you could see the bright blue sky for miles. The place was massive and had grass that reached way over our heads. I had never seen anything like it, it was so beautiful I felt like we were in another place. I honestly can't recall if the tall grass was wheat but that would make sense given it was so high over our heads. One day we ventured into the prairies, farther than we had ever gone before. After what seemed like 30 minutes of walking, we could see water. We raced to the edge, wanting to go for a swim but quickly realized the body of water was huge and we had no idea how deep it was. I connected the dots though and realized this is the same river that went across the edge of my back yard. It was kind of mind-blowing for a kid my age to realize how big a body of water can be and to picture the path the river takes.

As beautiful as the prairies were if I let my imaginative brain get the better of me, I could also imagine it to be a place where secrets could be kept, where you could do things, you didn't want anyone else to know about. You could hide a body out there, commit murder out there, kidnap someone and hold them hostage out there or have a cult like in Stephen King's book made into the Children of the Corn movie series. Even though in Children of the Corn, the psycho kids hung out between the rows of corn our prairies still reminded me enough of the corn fields for me to make the jump in my mind. You could hide in the prairies too because the grass was so high and if you knew the area by heart, you could definitely sneak up on someone without them knowing because the open area made it easy for the wind to whip through and you wouldn't be able to hear anything else. That's what happened when we were on our way back towards the dirt road one day, at first it was peaceful and quiet, then the wind blew and we couldn't hear anything. At the time my imagination got the better of me and I wondered what we would do if a bear or a wolf was standing in one of the rows. I tried to stay brave and not think about that too much, we were both fast runners so I figured we could get away. We could even climb a tree if we could reach the dirt road. Next thing you know we were face to face with a gigantic machine. It had a grill in the front that turned and looked like it would tear our little bodies to shreds. We ran and screamed down the rows of tall grass, but the machine kept coming and seemed to turn when we turned.

If we hadn't turned to look behind us at the right moment, that harvester would have torn us to pieces and our blood would have been sprayed all over the tall grass before we could even yell "Stop". Thankfully that didn't happen, and the driver saw us in time, but it did scare the shit out of us!

The machine finally came to a stop and a man jumped down from it. I didn't even see him before because the machine was so big and tall. He probably didn't see us at first either. Anyway, here we go again with an adult getting mad at us for being where they thought we shouldn't be. He asked us what we were doing there. He seemed pretty upset and told us we shouldn't be there because we could get hurt. We realized that now, but I wasn't up for someone telling me I couldn't go there anymore. The area was just too alluring, the freedom, the feeling of being in another place, another world. I just couldn't give that up. After the guy saw us a couple more times, he told us the day or days of the week that he is there with his machine so that we wouldn't risk getting hurt again. That worked for me.

Gwen and I choose to see the beautiful side of the prairies rather than the ominous and potentially dangerous side of the prairies. It was much more fun to imagine positive, exciting adventures that might lead to treasure than to think about the scary things. Not too hard for me and my ADHD, usually when I thought of something scary, it was gone as quick as it entered my mind because it was just my imagination, it wasn't real.

We spent a lot of time there over the next few years and even skated on the ponds in the winter. In the summer, we would occasionally see a few kids in the baseball diamond, and less on the dirt road but no one seemed to go to 'the prairies'. Were Gwen and I simply braver than most kids, or was there a real reason to be afraid?

I visited there years later and was disappointed to see the dirt road grown in and was now impassable. Maybe that was for the best, though, like sealing my precious memories in a timecapsule.

Chapter 7

A Bit About my Family

I didn't feel like my dad was overly engaged with me as a child...not sure if that was because he didn't want to admit I was different or that he didn't want to deal with teachers and people complaining about my behavior.

My dad is the youngest child born in his family, my mom the youngest female. She had one younger brother; all other siblings were older. My mom's father died when she was in high school. As you can imagine, life was difficult for my mom those last few years while my would-be grandfather was sick. A couple of her oldest brothers were already out of the house and making a living, and the rest of her family lived in a small house in Nashwaaksis. I was in that house many times because my nana lived there until her passing when she was 80 years old. Nana never re-married, she dedicated her life to raising her family and was the reason my mother's family stayed close. The importance of family was ingrained in my mother's and her siblings' minds. Even though most of us lived in the same city, Nana made sure we all purposefully got together for every birthday, at Thanksgiving and especially over Christmas. With 6 other siblings and all of their children, of which there are 15, we got together a lot!

I don't think it would be a stretch to say that my mom's older brothers felt a sense of needing to stand up for the family and to take on a bit of a fatherly role after their father's passing.

One of my mom's older brothers was an accountant, another owned his own business. I think their opinions on life, on being respectable and being successful highly influenced how the rest of the family saw those things and molded the rest of the family's behavior around what good and normal meant. Deviations from core beliefs were deemed to be judged as odd, weird and not fitting in.

Being the youngest female in her family, I have no doubt that what my mother's siblings thought was very important to her, and I think when life went awry, my mom would be stressed and may have led to unhappiness from time to time.

My dad only had 1 sibling, an older brother. His parents were more unique than most in that his father was almost 20 years older than his mother. They met when she was 18 and he was 36. Neither of them were married previously and Grampy was not the only one among his siblings, of which there were 13, that waited until later in life to get married. Their family worked on farms so worked long days and didn't have a lot of opportunity to meet someone special. My grandmother lost her mom one her first day of school and since her dad had to work, grammy was raised by her aunts.

As with anyone on earth, the way you were raised has an influence on how you will raise your children, what morals and beliefs you instill in your family and how you will parent and deal with the experiences your children present to you. Having two daughters and knowing how to care for and be affectionate to them was probably completely foreign to my dad and quite possibly terrifying!

My dad knew how to discipline, he knew how to take care of business and take care of us financially, he was a great handyman and helped to plan and build several of our houses while I was growing up. He wanted my sister and I to do well and to go to university. He liked to laugh and joke around, and he was a firefighter who later became a captain. I used to love walking over and showing up unannounced to my dad's work and he always seemed happy to see me. He would show me around the firehouse, showed me the trucks, the kitchen, where they slept and where the crew hung out when they weren't on a call. I have always been proud of my dad; I thought he had the coolest and bravest job. I felt like he was a superhero because he risked his life every day, he was at the station to save other people.

Dad also had a second job. He painted houses as a side job, so the family had extra money if needed. My dad enjoyed having a decent yard to play in and had either flower or vegetable gardens at most of the houses we lived in. He was always proud of having a well-manicured lawn with well placed flowers and bushes to liven it up. Until recently, and for as long as I can remember, my dad had a love of antique cars, and he owned and sold several since I was a child. Because of my dad, I truly appreciate antique cars. I used to have a poster in my room of a red and a bright yellow Lamborghini. I also loved the 60's corvette with all the curves, I also like the look of a Rolls Royce and would love to someday own an antique truck where the hood and front bumper curve.

My mom didn't work when my sister and I were in school, like a lot of other mothers at that time. She prepared meals, cleaned the house and was there when we got home from school. She would clean us up if we got hurt and nurse us when we were sick. She was a great time manager, and got my sister and I to appointments, to our after-school activities, to birthday parties and gatherings. She kept us fed, she kept us dressed, she kept us organized.

Both of my parents were loving in their way, but they were also judgemental if they thought you weren't making the right decisions, if you weren't living up to their standards.

In addition, there was my sister who had to compete for my parents' attention in a world where I sucked all the air out of the room. It's probably no surprise that her resentment of me grew.

Something that I always struggled with is that my parents never talked to me about important things – like the people and places to watch out for, or the very confusing time of puberty. I felt I was on my own in learning about all that, and I think a bit of conversation would have gone a long way. Maybe they just raised me the way they were raised. Or maybe they thought those were inappropriate topics to discuss with a child. Either way, I could have used a little more guidance.

Chapter 8

The Incidents

As mentioned, I was known by the older kids because we had the best sliding hill in town. That can sometimes turn out to be a bad thing. I believe this was the first tipping point for me, would I become what the adults already thought of me, or would I take this "experience" and have something good come out of it? How do you think it went?

There was a family that lived a few houses down from me. All the kids were older than me by quite a few years, so when the oldest showed interest in hanging out with me, I was really excited. I felt cool, special...why else would a kid 6 or 7 years older than me want to hang out? I was wrong, so wrong. To this day I still feel the shame. I was mad at myself and at my parents for not protecting me. I was mad at God too, but we'll get back to that.

Her name was Ophelia. She was a bigger girl with curly blond hair. She started being nice, just saying hello. Then she got talking to me at bit, giving me compliments. I now recognize these behaviours as 'grooming'. And one day, she asked me if I wanted to go to her house to hang out. I asked my parents, and I remember them being skeptical, wondering why a kid that age wanted to hang out with a kid my age. That of course made me mad, because I thought they were insulting me. My naivete made me say, "Why wouldn't she want to hang out with me?" It must have worked because they let me go.

Ophelia lived in one of the neat looking houses, all stone on the outside and it even had a turret that made me think of Rapunzel. It was a large split entry, and at the back of the house was a large wooden deck that overlooked the huge pond that I could see from my backyard. The kitchen was in the back, next to a stairwell going to the basement. I thought it was so cool because it was hidden. I love hidden spaces, hidden rooms, different types of ceilings etc. The more surprises and turns, the more alluring a place was to me. In my mind, it was like exploring an old mansion, with twisting staircases and hidden rooms, a great adventure.

It wasn't hard to lure me to the basement - I wanted to see what else there was to see. I wondered how many other kids had been in this house; how many got to see all the cool things I was about to see. Not many, I imagined. We got to the basement and the back wall was wood paneled. I had never seen that before, so I thought it was cool. At the bottom was a typical heat register, and aside from that, I don't remember much else about that room. But I do remember what happened there.

I asked Ophelia what she wanted to do, and she asked me if I wanted to do what all the older kids did (again, grooming). This made me feel special, like I was going to learn secrets that other kids my age didn't know. She told me to take down my pants and my underwear, and to lay on the floor next to the register – not what I had expected. My primary worry, though, was that someone might come down the stairs and see us. Ophelia assured me nobody was going to see me, and that we were going to have fun.

I believed her, trusted her even, so I did what she asked. I lay on the floor wondering what was going to happen. I was curious, but I wasn't scared. I should have been.

She came in close to my front bum (the term for vagina in my house...) which made me cover myself with my hands. I still wasn't scared, but I couldn't figure out why anyone would want to go near where I pee and poop. Innocence, right?

She talked to me then for a second and tried to move my hands out of the way. She told me to relax, and that I would like it. After a little coaxing, I released my hands, and she spread my legs apart. I shut my eyes tight, not knowing what she was going to do. She went down there with her tongue, and it really tickled. At least she wasn't hurting me. She continued for a bit, and I am ashamed to say that it did feel good. I stopped her several times, thinking someone was coming down the stairs, though no one ever did. I was super uncomfortable and after a very short while, I got up and was hoping we were going to do something else. I never got to 'completion', I didn't even know there was more to feel, or a particular ending I was supposed to come to.

Instead of moving on to something else, Ophelia said it was my turn to do it to her. I didn't want to, I was scared, nervous, confused. I had no idea what I was supposed to do. She of course reassured me and told me she would help me, tell me what to do... wasn't that nice of her.

Why didn't I run out of there? Even at her relatively young age, Ophelia knew how to reel me in. I was flattered that someone older wanted to hang out with me, and I wanted to learn about things other kids my age didn't know about, the secrets of what all the older kids did. So, I did it. She guided me, talked me through it. I didn't like doing it at all. It was so weird, and I almost threw up. Again, I stopped several times thinking someone was coming down the stairs, and again she assured me there wasn't. She moaned, "don't stop", but I couldn't keep going. I'm sure she was frustrated that I stopped, but she seemed ok and said that I should probably go home. I didn't want to stop hanging out, but she did, so I left. Before I left though, she told me not to tell anyone, especially my parents. I asked her why and she said it was our secret – and friends kept secrets for each other.

There was that friend word again. She had me, and I really wanted to remain friends. Even though I had a million emotions and thoughts going through my head, I kept the secret. I didn't tell anyone...even my best friend, Gwen. A few days later, Ophelia asked me to come over again - I said yes. I imagine you know what happened next - same place, same thing. Despite my protests, she wanted to do it again, and promised we could stop if I didn't like it. I wanted to make her happy, so I thought of ways to do it without feeling like I was going to throw up. Maybe having a drink with me would make it better? She gave me a tall glass of orange juice, with pulp. To this day, orange juice with pulp makes me gag.

She said I had to start first because the last time, I quit before something 'happened'. I tried; I did. I took sips of orange juice, but it wasn't enough. I stopped, and Ophelia wasn't happy. I felt like a failure; she told me to go home and again, not to tell anyone.

I cried all the way home. I had let Ophelia down, and I assumed the short-lived friendship, if you can call it that, was over. Well, it wasn't. At least not yet.

It took about a couple of weeks before she talked to me again. Once again, she invited me to her house. I told her I wasn't interested if we would be doing the same thing. She assured me we were going to do something different. She had me again, man I was gullible. We were going to do something different mind you, so I guess there's that.

We went to a different room this time, a bedroom upstairs where a window faced the street. I felt like Ophelia was prepping me for something. She was asking if I liked the feeling from before and if I had ever done this or that. The answers of course where all no, I was like 10 for fuck's sake. Her brother then entered the room.

He was a good-looking guy, tall, brown hair, big brown eyes. I knew him from the neighborhood but never said more than hi to him before. He looked at me and smiled, then talked to his sister to see if she had mentioned what we were going to do. She said she hadn't gotten that far. There was a different dynamic now, a different feel to the room with him being there and I was actually a little scared. I knew what Ophelia and I tried, and I knew that a boy had something else down there, but I couldn't imagine what new thing we'd be doing.

I told them I should go home, that I forgot my mom was waiting for me, but they didn't want me to go. The more I tried to leave, the more they pushed for me to stay, so naturally I got more and more nervous. Ophelia kept saying it would be ok. She told me to pull down my pants like I had for her. I can't recall if I obliged or if Ophelia did it for me, but her brother started to undo his belt buckle. I stood in front of them both, pants and panties pulled down for all to see. Behind me there was a bed.

Ophelia's brother was surprised because I had no hair down there. Again, I was 10. He looked at Ophelia and asked her how old I was. She said she didn't know, and then he turned and asked me. I told him and he wasn't impressed. He started saying something about me being too young and Ophelia got frustrated. In her anger, over displeasing her brother, Ophelia yelled at me to go home. I was out

27

of there so fast; I don't remember descending the outside staircase or running to my yard.

When I got to my yard, I started crying, trying to process what had happened and what could have happened. As I stood there, I recalled Ophelia's last words to me, "You better not tell anyone about this – what we were doing was bad, and we'll all get into big trouble".

Stupid, scared, confused and angry – that's how I felt. I was completely devastated. Why were we doing something we weren't supposed to?

I had all these feelings and questions, but I couldn't talk to anyone. I was so lost. I considered myself a good kid – I went to church and Sunday School, I listened to my parents, I came from a respectable family. Now, I was the bad kid - I was every bad thing anyone had ever thought of me.

Still in my front yard, I looked around at the lush grass, beautiful trees and colourful flower beds. What should have been beautiful seemed dull to me – because nothing made any sense. I decided that since I couldn't tell anyone, I would talk to God. I was going to lash out at him for letting something like that happen to me. I knew I dodged a bullet, and I knew it could have been so much worse. The incident played over and over in my mind – and the belief that I was now a 'bad kid' changed me. It really changed me. Why had God let that happen to me? Wasn't he supposed to protect us? I just couldn't understand, and I came to the only logical conclusion I could at the time. I stopped believing in God.

Chapter 9

The Best Teacher

Since I chose to stop believing in God, I became darker, more sarcastic. I kept my head down and was quieter than normal. I was also angry, and hated people who lied, or teased me, or made me conspicuous with their comments or jokes.

It also made me question what my purpose was in life. This may seem like a normal thing to do, but not for a middle-school kid. I felt like I was just moving through life, purposeless, unimportant, invisible.

My fourth-grade teacher was the only light in my life during the school day. Mr. Beaulieu had black hair, a mustache, a thin build and the kindest eyes. He had a small thin nose and was quite handsome by my standards. He was the kind of teacher that really cared and really tried - and I was lucky enough to have him in Grade 6 too. He liked me and seemed to understand that I wasn't a bad kid. He had noticed that I had changed, he asked me if everything was ok and told me he was there if I ever wanted to talk.

Unfortunately, I was really on edge and was quick to jump to conclusions. One day he decided to point something out about me, something funny, I can't totally remember what it was, but I remember the kids in my class laughing and I was livid. How could the perfect teacher, my favourite teacher, do that to me? I gave him a look that could have cut right through his soul. He was surprised by my reaction because he was just trying to be funny, but it was too soon after the 'incidents' and I was in no laughing mood. I felt like he betrayed the special bond we had, and I stopped speaking to him. It only lasted a couple of weeks, but that's a long time when you're a kid.

No matter my attitude or behaviours, he never gave up on me. He tried to get me to smile or laugh at something every day. I actually think I hurt his feelings, but he wouldn't give up on me. He was the kind of teacher I wish every teacher was like, what every teacher should be.

With all of Mr. Beaulieu's efforts to make things the way they used to be between us, I broke. One day he said something off the cuff, I don't remember what he said but it made me smile and he looked at me with that sweet, sincere face and he smiled too. I actually tried to stop smiling right away, I was mad at myself for giving in and for letting my guard down, like I was betraying myself. I needed to have a hard shell now, right?

After that, things between me and Mr. Beaulieu were pretty much the same as they were before the 'incidents'. I trusted him and didn't feel like I needed to be closed off to him.

I actually considered telling Mr. Beaulieu about the 'incidents', but I just couldn't. The thought of him looking at me differently once he heard what happened was enough to keep me quiet. I wonder what would have happened if I had told him. I wonder if the parents or the brother and sister would be questioned and arrested. I often wonder if I could have saved other young girls and boys, in my neighborhood, from the same fate or from something worse. Guilt is an awfully heavy thing, and I feel it to this day. I often wonder if any of the kids in my neighborhood had worse fates, things that may have happened that you can't come back from. I know that wondering about things that you can't know about is futile but that doesn't stop our wonderful brains from going there, does it?

There is only one negative thing about me acting normal again with Mr. Beaulieu, he never asked me again about how my behavior had changed for a while and what may have caused it.

Chapter 10

The Long Walk Home

Even though things were good with Mr. Beaulieu and me again, I still felt pretty alone. I didn't feel any connection with the kids in my class, so I decided to see if I could find friendships with the English kids during lunches and recesses. The first day I tried this, it was awkward because the English kids went out the far side doors and the French kids went out the doors at the other end of the school. Even the school had separated English and French kids! So, I had to go through all these kids in the hall, just to get to the 'other side'. Some of the English kids didn't like me being in their space, saying I didn't belong there. Others stood up for me, though, so it was good for a short while.

As mentioned, the perception was that the English kids were tougher, had more life experience. Because of that, I did feel more connected to them. I could be vulgar without kids looking at me like I was bad. It was more natural to the English kids, so I felt more comfortable around them. The French kids were more innocent, sheltered. After the 'incidents' I just couldn't relate to them, mostly because I could no longer pretend everything was great and innocent.

I made friends with a couple of guys in English who were around my age, which for me seemed to be easier to do then making friends with girls. I guess I was a tomboy. We hung out at lunchtime and at recesses for a couple of months and all seemed great. One day they mentioned to me that one of their dads wanted to meet me, because he didn't believe that his kid was friends with a girl, or maybe with a girl in French Immersion... I didn't think a whole lot of it, just thought it was something mentioned in passing.

32

However, over the following weeks they mentioned it more and more.

It started to get a bit weird, and I thought to myself, "I'm not allowed to go to a boy's house". I was still only 10 years old. I told them no, then they asked if I would be able to walk home with them, as their house was only 5 minutes from the school. They also said that my parents didn't have to know.

My hackles were up now, I thought, "Why would some kid's dad want to meet me?" And, of course, I thought of the 'incidents'. A couple of days later, they told me that it was happening that day and that I was not to take the bus home. They were not going to take no for an answer. I was stressed the rest of the day, and I was trying to think of excuses as to why I couldn't go.

I told them I wasn't 'feeling well', and that my mom expected me to come off the bus near our house. I said she'd be worried if I wasn't there, and that she might come looking for me. They didn't seem to care, and the desperation in their actions had me scared.

At the end of the school day, I rushed to where the bus always picked me up and hid behind some kids in line. I wanted to get on that bus so bad, but the driver wasn't letting kids on yet as he was chatting away with another bus driver. He didn't know how badly I needed to get on that bus, or that my nerves were about to fry my whole body. How would he know?

The boys found me.

They pulled me by my arms and took me out of the line. I protested, but not fiercely enough because no one seemed to notice, not even the teachers on bus duty. I guess that's what happens in big schools, too many faces in a sea of kids, so things go unnoticed. My mind was racing a mile a minute, "how am I going to get out of this?" A thought popped into my head, I told them I forgot something in the school and that I had to go get it first. They let me go back in the school but wanted to follow me. I said that was stupid, and that I would be right back. I went into the school and ran up a flight of stairs that led to a door to the outside. That's where kids would beat the chalkboard erasers to clean them every day. There was a little landing as soon as you opened the door then stairs back down to the ground. I hid there, checking every minute or so to see when my bus started to leave, my plan was to run down when I saw it moving without the two boys noticing and draw the bus driver's attention so he would stop, and I'd be safe.

I must have been sitting there a little too long, because the boys went in the school to look for me. They discovered my hiding place, just as I watched my bus, my safety plan, turn out of the school driveway and into the street. I was crushed.

The boys were not happy that I tried to ditch them. I told them I was nervous about getting in trouble at home, which seemed to calm things a bit, but I knew I still had to get away. I told them to wait while I went to the bathroom. When I entered the school this time, though, the door locked behind me and they couldn't get in. Finally, a break! I ran to the principal's office and told the secretary I missed my bus - she let me call home for a ride. I called my mom but only told her I missed the bus – I must have been too scared to say what was really going on. My mom was annoyed that I missed the bus and questioned me as to how it happened. She said she couldn't come to get me, and that I would have to walk home.

WTF? Was this tough love? A form of punishment? A lesson to be learned?

I was trapped. I couldn't bring myself to say what really happened, and my mother was reacting to only partial information. I told her I was scared, "what if I get lost?", to no avail - she had no idea of the situation I had found myself in. Once again, I was on my own and forced to think my way out of a difficult situation. I was crying by then, fear overtaking me, I even asked the few adults left in the school if they could possibly drive me home. They were too preoccupied with getting home themselves, to see I was scared and needed help.

It was getting late, but I thought if I stayed there long enough, they would just give up and go home. If I stayed too long, though, I would have ended up walking home alone in the dark – which wasn't really a better option. After 5 or 10 minutes, I went back outside - and I didn't see them. I was relieved, and I started the long trek home. My relief was short-lived, though, as they spotted me at the end of the school driveway. I couldn't believe they had waited. I was already scared, and the fact that they had waited scared me even more... I thought, "what the heck is wrong with them?" It just wasn't 'normal' behavior. My next plan was simple – I ran and ran and ran. I was fast, one of the fastest kids in my school, but what I had in speed I lacked in stamina. They caught me, ironically right in front of the church I went to (but didn't believe in...). I had only made it a few streets away from the school.

I was freaking out, but not so they could see. I asked them why they were doing this me – I said, "I thought we were friends". They said we were friends and that they only wanted to prove to one of their dad's that they weren't making me up. I couldn't understand why that was so important to them and I told them the dad should just believe them. They tried to make me go with them, and I had the feeling we were close to wherever they wanted to take me. It was at this point I had had enough. I asked them why they wanted me to get in trouble with my family. I said that friends don't do that to each other, and that if they didn't let me go home, then I would no longer be friends with them.

I don't know why or how, but that seemed to strike a chord with them. They may have simply been exhausted, just as I was. All this wasted time, chasing a kid who was hiding, fleeing, protesting, fighting. Sensing an opportunity, I asked them how they would feel if I got lost, or if something bad happened to me on the way home. I told them I was already mad that they made me miss my bus, and that it was a long way home for me without a drive. Somehow, appealing to them as a person seemed to be working.

They let me go.

I couldn't believe it! I was so relieved, so happy that I started running again, at least for a while. I made it home without any further issues. My elation didn't last long, as my mom was still mad at me – she thought I was late on purpose. I was so mad. And I let her know it too, pointing out that something bad could have happened to me, just because she wouldn't pick me up. I think that scared her a bit. I know she was unaware of the situation I was in, but I still felt she shouldn't have let me walk home alone.

I thought about what happened, and what could have happened, a lot that night. Even though I could only imagine what could have happened, I naturally thought about the 'incidents'. I had strong instincts and self-preservation - if I had been naïve, or hadn't had the experience of the 'incidents', I might have gone with them, and who knows what might have happened.

I stopped being friends with them. Immediately. Fuck with me and we're done.

They didn't deserve my friendship, and there was no way I would ever trust them again. I think they were sad, but they knew they had gone too far. After that, I kinda stuck in the middle of the school yard, not really hanging with the French or the English kids. I was just… there. Staying under the radar, watching others run

36

around and play. I eventually started hanging out more with the French guys who were into sports, because I was athletic too. I figured this would be better than just standing around, and that time would pass by faster. They knew I was athletic, because they were in my gym class. Things were better for a while – we played baseball, ran around – they even started inviting me along (instead of me just hanging around hoping they would let me join them). I think they liked having a girl or two hanging around, especially ones who were as athletic as they were and I enjoyed it too.

Grade 4 was over, and it was finally summer.

Chapter 11 Gymnastic Days

Having ADHD certainly made some aspects of life more difficult for me, as well as for my family, teachers and probably my friends. As mentioned, I only had a couple of friends at school. After school and on weekends, there was always Gwen. I think a lot of people didn't know how to deal with me, and I think a lot of kids were scared of me, perhaps they thought I was too unpredictable or that they couldn't handle all the energy I gave off. I was always moving, mostly shaking one or both legs. Oddly though, I could watch tv for hours if it was captivating for me. The Bugs Bunny and Scooby-Doo shows were among my favourites.

One thing that helped me release excess energy was gymnastics. I absolutely loved to jump, swing, tumble... My favorite gymnastics equipment was the bars and the mat. I took lessons twice a week at one of the local elementary schools, and I was hooked. I even got Gwen to join.

Sticking with the lessons for about four years, one of my instructors suggested that if I wanted to further improve, I would have to go to another gymnastics facility. I was told about a more advanced gymnastics club on the other side of the river, and I was both surprised and honoured that they saw potential in me. I was sad to be leaving everyone I knew, but I did love gymnastics, and I wanted to see what else I could learn.

The place was on the Southside, it was huge and there were a lot of people there. Kids were separated by age, and I was feeling intimated watching what the others could do. I really wanted to be as good as them and of course to make new friends... unfortunately that wasn't in the cards. I only lasted there about a month and a half.

It started off ok. I was a bit shy but befriended one of the girls fairly quickly - she was great. For many reasons, I wish what happened didn't happen. I lost a friend, I lost my confidence, and I lost gymnastics. I couldn't show my face at the new club again, and I couldn't go back to my old gymnastics group either.

It was about the third week at the new place. One of my new teachers told my group that we would have to come up with our own individual floor routine and perform it in front of the class. We never had to do anything like that at my old gymnastics school. The thought of having to come up with a routine, with my ADHD brain and no help, made me want to leave then and there. It was then I realised how far behind my former gymnastics place was in their teaching – not that it was any fault of theirs. I really felt I did not belong with this new group, and I was embarrassed by my inability to do a back handspring. It got to me, with negative self-talk and fear soon taking over.

I decided to try to come up with a routine, and I was determined that it would include a back handspring. One day in my living room, I convinced myself I was going to do it. I got myself hyped up and tried, and when I finally 'did it' for the first time, it was more of a backflip than a back handspring. I tried over and over again, readjusting, jumping higher and trying to do it faster, draining all of my energy. On my final attempt, I managed to land on my face, giving myself carpet burn on my cheek. That was it, I was done. Never did manage to really do a back handspring.

The new gymnastics club was causing me a lot of stress. I didn't want to be a quitter, and that was really the only thing that kept me from quitting. Just to complicate things, my body started to experience changes around that time as well. Not full-blown puberty, just the fun changes, like sweating. And yes, as hard as it is to imagine, those two things are related, and conspired together to make me the center of attention again, and not in a good way.

It might have been physical exertion; it might have been the stress of my non-existing floor routine. Either way, I was sweating, and it smelled bad. Oniony, to the best of my recollection. I noticed the odour but said nothing. I just turned my nose up thinking it was someone else. Others weren't as subtle as I was. They were determined to find out who the stink was coming from, and they started smelling each other's pits. I wasn't going to let anyone near my pits, so I smelled myself.

I was mortified. It was me.

I didn't understand why this was happening, and I wondered if I could hide it. Obviously, it was a bit late for that strategy, they could already smell it. Kids can be mean, asking questions such as, "Ever hear of deodorant?". Of course I had, but no one ever told me I would need it then. That was my parents' job, and I was so mad at them for not doing their job! Thank goodness this embarrassment came close to the end of the practice. After some good laughs, and a bit more ridicule, I walked out of that class for the last time.

I was crushed, and my dreams of becoming a great gymnast were circling the drain. I begged my mother to let me quit. I was mortified and never wanted to go back there again. I just couldn't show my face there. At least, being a Northsider, I didn't go to school with these kids. Soon, all would be forgotten. Not by me of course, but by others, I am sure it was just a blip on their radar.

I never went back to gymnastics, not really. I tried for a few months when I was in junior high, but my heart was never in it. To this day I regret it, though I still get some joy from watching Olympic events. Maybe it reminds me what it felt like to be really good at something – like I felt when I was doing gymnastics on the Northside. I do wish my parents, or really anyone, would have encouraged me more. I wish they told me I was really good. Or to hold my head high and to never give up.

I wish someone said something... anything. But no one did.

Chapter 12

The Local Pool

Gymnastics was done, now what was I to do with all my excess energy? In the summers, that question was easily answered. I went to the pool. Summers, as a kid, were the best. Fun was never far away, put on your bathing suit, grab a towel and start walking. Back then there was no talk of sunscreen, or mention that you should only be out in the sun for short periods of time. We'd be out all afternoon, sometimes longer. I was so tanned by the end of the summer, some kids wondered if I was part Indigenous, or Black.

From my house, it was a short walk to hang out at the local pool. Kids would go to that huge, rectangular pool every nice day of the summer. It had a shallow end, a deep end, and a diving board with a concrete deck bordering it. There was lots of space to lay out your towel and get a tan.

I loved it when my dad went to the pool. He was an amazing swimmer and diver, and he always did tricks off the diving board. I remember the kids calling out tricks for him to do – dives, cannonballs, flips and 'Johnny Ass-Cracker's. For those who don't know, a 'Johnny Ass-Cracker' is a move where you jump off the diving board with your arms holding one leg bent to your chest with the other leg out long. If you leaned back slightly, you could

41

make a huge splash. Other kids in other towns called this a 'can opener', guess every group of kids had different names for things.

My dad loved the attention, and he took great delight in making huge splashes to soak everyone. Because of dad, a lot of kids at the pool came to know who I was too, which made me feel pretty cool. Dad showed me some of his favourite moves, so as he went to the pool less and less, I kind of took over in the 'trick' department.

As I got a bit older, my parents allowed me to walk to the pool without them. We all headed to the pool on those hot days - I was usually one of the first kids starting out, then I'd meet up with a friend or two. We'd also pick up some stragglers along the way and there were always others that joined us. It was like we were a little drove of worker bees all heading to the same place picking up more along the way. Although I felt grown up walking to the pool, there were some occurrences that shook me to my core.

Some days while walking to the pool, I noticed a plain white van driving or parking on one of the streets in my neighbourhood. It caught my eye because there were no advertisements on it, and all of the windows were heavily tinted. It had the typical big two doors that opened at the back like a delivery van. I remember wondering what they were doing parked on the side of the road, it just wasn't common to see vehicles parked on that street, which was one of the main streets in the area.

One seemingly-normal sunny day, a couple of kids and I were walking to the pool. We turned a corner, only to witness a scary scene. The van was there, but our attention was on a young boy who was trying to get away from two adult men. The boy was around seven years old; he was thin with short brown hair, wearing a bathing suit and carrying a towel just like the rest of us kids.

We passed the boy and men, continuously stopping and looking back. The boy was pleading for our help, "Please help me, they're trying to take me". He seemed so scared. One of the men assured us it was all a joke, and that we should move along. Hesitantly, we started to leave but the terror in that boy's voice gave me a feeling in my gut that was so strong, I knew something was off. Why would the boy be that scared if he knew them? We thought maybe they were family, that the boy was scared because they abused him. I told my friends that this didn't seem normal - thankfully they agreed, and we turned back to help the young boy.

When we got back to the scene, the tone had changed. The men told us to leave and to mind our own business. At this point, my instincts were on high-alert, and I was getting mad. I questioned the men, who insisted they were just taking the boy home – but that's not what it looked like. They were trying to shove him in the back of the van, while he desperately resisted – we grabbed the boy's arm to help him escape. So, there we were, four kids in bathing suits, carrying towels and trying to foil what appeared to be a kidnapping.

The commotion alerted a close-by neighbour, and we screamed to him that we needed help. The neighbour stayed in his yard, likely unclear what was going on or if it was a dangerous situation. The men told the neighbour the same story they told us kids, which seemed to work because he went back inside his house. It was back to us kids versus the men. We got the boy free, and he ran – making one of the men very angry. He charged toward us, trying to grab one of us, any of us. Terrified, we then knew for sure they were up to no good and made our way toward one of the houses. The angry man tried to grab me, but I was spunky, and I twisted away from his grasp. At this point, the other man sensed too much time had passed, saying it wasn't worth it and that they should leave. Finally, they got back in their van and did just that. The boy hugged me hard, crying. I told him he would never have to walk alone again; he could walk with us anytime. Remarkable how wisdom can even come to a pre-pubescent kid when certain situations present themselves.

After the white-van-kidnap-attempt, a lot of houses in the neighbourhood started putting signs in their windows – Neighbourhood Watch. What the sign meant, was that a kid could feel safe going to the home if they were in trouble, hurt or scared. It was great.

The other development, which made me feel important, was that people in the area would offer us a lift to the pool if they saw us walking. The offers of help were genuine, not creepy. We'd sit away from the driver, like in the box of a truck. I think our record, for most kids piled in the box of a truck, was twelve. It was exciting and fun, like summers were supposed to be. We'd get dropped off at the local fire station and run across the field to the pool. The authorities didn't seem too interested in a bunch of kids in the back of a truck, and this was before seatbelt laws came in.

I often wondered about that van, though we never saw it again. Did they move on to another neighbourhood? Did they try to take other kids? Innocently, I really didn't understand why men would want to take a boy, or what might have happened to him had they been successful. I did, though, have a strong feeling that if they had gotten the boy into the van, we'd never have seen him again.

Chapter 13

The New Boy

I was looking forward to a new schoolyear, Grade 5 was a new beginning. There was a boy in my class named James, who came from a different city. He had a bigger build than most of the guys in my class and looked more athletic. He had light brown hockey-hair and glasses. Hockey-hair, for non-Canadians, is also called a mullet - long in the back, short in the front. He was loud, boisterous, funny, utterly annoying and really cute.

He didn't live that far from me but still went on a different bus. He had a quirky, loud laugh that was infectious - you couldn't help but laugh too. Not sure if he was funny at his old school, or if it was his way of quickly making friends and fitting in. Either way, it worked.

At times, James could be cruel and hurt people's feelings. Not sure how bullies choose their targets, but a few months into school he decided I was his. He would use any little thing to draw negative attention to me. He'd walk past me in art class, point at my drawing and start laughing hysterically. It made me so self-conscious that I wouldn't let anyone else see it. If I tripped, he'd laugh. If I missed a throw, he'd laugh. If I missed hitting the ball, he'd laugh…you get the picture. I didn't know what I did to make him hate me so much.

The schoolyear went on, and I grew tired of James and his jokes. I decided to confront him, I wanted to know why he hated me.

I felt I had my chance when the teacher left the room but was distracted by the chatter in the room – something about '5 minutes in heaven'. I was still so naïve in some ways; I had no idea what they meant.

There was a vestibule on the right-hand side of the classroom where we hung our jackets. The girl who was talking about '5 minutes in heaven' told me that James wanted to go in there with me. I certainly didn't know why he would want to do that, and assumed it was to embarrass me somehow. I said no. I was not going in there with him. She told me that he liked me, but I didn't believe her. He had been so mean to me most of the year, it just didn't make sense. It occurred to me though that if I went in there with him, I could confront him. So, I went in.

Someone stood by the door to the classroom and watched the hall to see when the teacher was coming back. In the vestibule, James started off with small talk, asking me how I was doing and being really nice. – it was so confusing. I just came out with it and asked him why he hated me and of course, he laughed. He said he didn't hate me, he liked me. He really liked me. I protested that he was just trying to make me look stupid, but he was adamant. So, I asked him why he was so mean to me.

"It was my way to get your attention," was his response.

I should probably describe myself a little more. I was slim, and had (still have) curly brown hair, dark hazel eyes and dark eyelashes. I also had flawless skin but didn't we all at that age. I guess you could say I was pretty. I probably didn't think so at the time, the 'incidents' had done a number on my self-esteem.

I knew I was alright, though, all the blemishes were on the inside, invisible to those around me. My attitude and sense of humor also helped to hide the flaws.

I told James that I liked him too and we were inseparable for a couple of years. I felt like things might actually be turning around for me. James was well-known and well-liked, and the kids in my classes seemed to find me more approachable. Although I didn't hang out with anyone outside my neighborhood after school, I felt like I finally had more than a couple of friends.

James and I had a lot of fun together, innocent fun. He used to be the neighborhood paperboy, and I used to walk around with him on his route. When he wasn't on his paper route, he would walk around the neighborhood with a huge boom-box on one shoulder, listening to all kinds of great music. He was so cool and confident. I had listened to a lot of pop music growing up, girls like Madonna and Cindy Lauper were among my favorites. James introduced me to rock music, including great bands like Bon Jovi (still a favourite), AC/DC, and Corey Hart (a Canadian artist who was huge in the 80's).

School life was getting better, except for our teacher. What a bag... I think it was her first-year teaching, and I have to admit, we weren't the easiest class to manage. I'm pretty sure no one really liked her because of the way she treated us – she did not like us, and wanted to be anywhere else in the world, at least that's how we felt. She was a bully.

Children have some crazy ideas, and they don't always get the answers right. Most teachers understand this, and they know how to encourage kids to grow – both personally and academically. Not her, she laughed when a student got the wrong answer and she encouraged the other students to respond similarly. WTF? Who does that to a kid? She is the reason I stopped answering questions in class. Think about that, she made young, impressionable students terrified to answer a question, terrified to be ridiculed by peers, peers she encouraged to ridicule. And it stuck – in junior high, I would look anywhere but at the teacher, hoping they wouldn't call on me to answer a question out loud in class. You'd think 'teacher's college' would have weeded out these miserable miscreants. If you can't lift up and encourage kids, you shouldn't be a teacher.

Then, the switcheroo. Just before the Christmas break, she made each student in her class a beautiful and delicate scene inside a hollowed-out boiled eggshell. I was in awe of its beauty, and more so taken aback by the care and time it would have taken to create such an intricate piece. Each piece must have taken hours, let alone all 22 of them.

I told her I was surprised by what she did. When she asked why, I was (of course) honest and blunt – "I thought you hated us." She was taken aback, I realise now. I explained that the laughing and making fun of us had created a certain dynamic in the room. I would argue this was an epiphany for her, as her effort and attitude were dramatically different for the remainder of the year.

As the schoolyear wound down, my teacher decided to play a game of spelling and math problems. There were prizes (treats I think) for correct answers, and additional rewards for the top few students. This was my introduction to hyper-focus, a byproduct of ADHD. I enjoyed competition in this way, and I guess the speed of having to come up with an answer had my brain firing well. We all knew who the 'smart kids' were, and even though I wouldn't have thought of myself that way, in this game I was giving the smart kids a run for their money.

The experience of that day was a double-edged sword. As fun as it was to see the amazed look on my classmate's faces, it also exposed that most of my classmates considered me among the bottom kids in terms of intelligence. Now, I get it. I was fidgety, had a short attention-span, got in some trouble… but it still hurt.

In your face, you judgemental pricks.

The schoolyear ended, and soon it was summer. Just two months before being in the highest (elementary) grade. Top of the food chain.

Chapter 14

I Can't Spend the Night

My birthday was early in the school year, and I decided to have a sleepover for my party. My parents gave me a limit on how many girls I could invite. I was genuinely surprised when the demand outstripped the supply – everyone wanted to come, including the most popular girls in French Immersion. I ended up inviting more than the number of people my parents wanted me to stick to, but not by much, and it wasn't too hard to convince them since I said I was finally making some friends. The sleepover was great, we watched a horror movie and most of the girls had pillows over their faces, but Gwen and I just sat there watching. We all pigged out on snacks, laughed and talked until early into the morning. That is one memory I still cherish.

Ironically… I threw great sleepovers, but I couldn't spend the night at anyone else's house. To this day, I would much rather make my way home then to sleep in someone else's place. Being ADHD, I couldn't sleep in. I woke, predictably, every day between 6 and 7 am. That's not an issue when you are in your own home, knowing you could get up, grab a bowl of cereal and watch tv. In someone else's home, I didn't feel like I could do that. My parents had taught me early on that you don't go into someone else's cupboards or their fridge. You asked them to get you what you wanted, and asked permission to do anything. Which is difficult if everyone's asleep…

Sleep itself was another issue. I could be having the time of my life, but when they announced 'bedtime', my anxiety went through the roof, and I would want my parents to pick me up. When it was time to go to sleep at a friend's house, the silence and knowing that I could no longer talk was more than I could bear.

The worst part was that I couldn't move.

What I mean by that is that I had to sit still, so my friend(s) could fall asleep. The problem with that is that I was a fidgeter, my legs were always going while awake, and I usually rocked myself to sleep. It was the only way to get rid of the excess energy, so I could relax and fall asleep. I know, weird, but that was a secret I wanted to keep to myself. I knew I would be judged if people found out my little secret.

Thanks to James, the more popular girls started paying more attention to me, talking to me. We would hang out at recess. I thought, wow, I finally have some girlfriends, and they are the popular kids. Samantha was the most popular kid in my grade; she had straight dark hair, almost black, that hung to her shoulders and was perfectly silky. She was of slim build and had a gap between her two front teeth. Her parents had money, and she always wore brand name clothes.

One day Samantha asked me to spend the night at her house on the upcoming weekend. I was excited, but also terrified because I had failed at every sleepover I had attempted so far. I told her that I would like to but had to ask my mom first. I went home not knowing what to do. I knew the stakes were high, if I could stay the night and we had fun then I would solidify my place amongst the popular kids. I also wondered if she would want to do things like the 'incidents', and what I would do if I found myself in that kind of situation again.

I wanted, if not needed, a bigger friend group so bad that I made the decision to go, despite my concerns. My mom warned me that she wouldn't come get me this time, mostly because it was on the other side of the river. So, I had to be sure that I wanted to go and that I could stay the night. I convinced both myself and my mom that I could do it.

I arrived at Samantha's house late afternoon on a Saturday. Her house was huge. When you walked in, there was a big entry way that led into the kitchen and at the back of the house was a staircase on both sides leading to the upstairs. Samantha's bedroom was up there. It was huge too, and her bed was a queen size. Mine was still a single bed.

The evening went great. We ate, we laughed, we watched tv and we even went in her pool (though it was cold). I couldn't believe how much fun I was having, and that Samantha and I were getting along so well. It felt like we had been friends for a while.

Evening turned to nighttime and with that a request from her mom for us to get ready for bed. I started to worry. Thoughts of how to relax and go to sleep were swimming in my head. We brushed our teeth, changed our clothes and then turned out the light. I was hoping we would talk deep into the night, and just fall asleep… without even trying to fall asleep.

It started out well. Samantha was feeding me gossip, not the nice kind, of course. I shouldn't have been surprised that she would know embarrassing things about some of the kids at school. She even told me that one girl in our class had spent the night at her house and had tried to do things similar to the 'incidents' with her. I felt bad for the girl Samantha was talking about. She lived near me, and I was pretty sure she had endured something like I had. It was the first time I heard about a girl being into girls, at least out loud. I don't think this girl was actually gay, though, because she certainly had boyfriends later on and got married. Someone probably fucked with her head too, making her think that was an appropriate way to behave at the time.

I must admit, I was happy that Samantha mentioned it to me, and that she was disgusted by it. That gave me the answer I had been wondering about. She didn't like that kind of stuff, and I was relieved because I didn't ever want to do that again. I wanted to forget those things had ever happened to me. Samantha then said she was tired and was going to sleep. I wasn't ready yet.

I tried, I really did, I probably tried for an hour. I had hoped I would just get exhausted and fall asleep, but my mind wouldn't shut off. I kept thinking about the morning, what if I woke up too early, what if I got hungry, what if I was bored and wanted to watch tv? Would Samantha be mad? Then I started thinking about going home, could I come back early in the morning? What if, what if, what if. I got myself into such a state that I convinced myself that I had to go home, that my mom would come get me, even though she said she wouldn't.

I started telling Samantha that I didn't feel good and that I had to go home. She told her mom, who questioned me – so I fibbed. I said my stomach hurt, and that I wanted to go home. I told them if I felt good in the morning that I would come back early, and we could still hang out all day and swim in her pool. It took a while for me to get them to allow me to call home and ask to be picked up. My mom was not impressed, and she refused for a while. I was trying to hold in my feelings, but I was basically beside myself – on autopilot, unwilling and unable to listen to reason.

My mom finally agreed to come get me. Samantha seemed understanding, and was nice the whole time, even though she really wanted me to stay. It must have been 1:30 in the morning by the time I got in the car. As soon as I was in and settled, I felt instant relief. My chest loosened; my mind settled...

And I fell asleep.

I woke up early the next morning and waited for an hour or so before calling Samantha. I told her how sorry I was that I couldn't spend the night. I told her I felt better and asked her if she wanted to hang out. She said maybe later. I was a bit worried but still felt ok because Samantha was still being nice. I called her later and no one answered. I tried one last time in the middle of the afternoon and she said it was getting too late, and that she would just see me at school the next day. I said OK and I assumed everything was fine, she was probably just a bit hurt. Nonetheless, I was a bit weary of what Monday morning might bring.

It wasn't until noon on Monday that I realized things weren't ok. The popular kids were in their regular place, near the badminton courts to the right of the school. I didn't know that before because I wasn't one of them. At noon hour I was invited to go to the court to hang out and I was pretty excited. There were at least 10 kids there, including James and Samantha.

As soon as Samantha saw me, she started yelling at me, asking what I was doing there. I was surprised by her reaction, and I felt a little sheepish. I told her I was there to hang out with them, but she said I wasn't allowed. I was flabbergasted. I looked around at everyone, trying to gauge how the rest of them felt. Although there were a couple looks of sympathy, James just shrugged instead of standing up for me, so that was that. I had pissed Samantha off for not spending the night, and now I was an outcast. She must have been hurt, but instead of talking to me about it, she decided to make me feel the same way – but more. I had been so close to popularity, but it came with strings that I couldn't tether to anything solid. This was the first time I was openly bullied by exclusion.

I later asked James why he hadn't helped me – he said he was afraid to be kicked out of the group too, so he did nothing. I was mad, but I understood. He was the new kid, in a good place with everyone, and didn't want to lose that.

I was on the outs again.

Chapter 15

The Worst News Ever

Sixth grade was over, summer had arrived, and my parents told my sister and I that we were moving. I was devastated. No more sliding hill, no more walking to the pool, and maybe no more Gwen and James?

That summer, I was full of emotions. Puberty had started, my little boobs were starting to show, and they hurt all the time. Gwen, being a year younger than me, was curious about the changes I was experiencing. I felt awkward about the transition to young adulthood and wanted to hide it, but she kept pressuring me to show her how we were different now. Although Gwen was innocent about it and we shared everything else, this part I couldn't share. It made me really uncomfortable, and I felt vulnerable again, like when the 'incidents' happened. I hurt her feelings, and I felt bad, but she didn't understand how my past had affected me. Things were a bit weird after that, then I moved, and we lost touch. We went to the same junior high school but she didn't get there until the next year and the school was huge, so we didn't really run into each other. We were both trying to navigate a new world. Over the years, I heard she got into some drinking and throwing parties.

I know she was just having fun, but I worried about her.

My ADHD made me do impulsive things, regardless of the consequences that certain actions might have. Additionally, I am also quite passionate. I'm not sure that is related to ADHD, but the combination was quite combustible. Regarding James, my feelings were already pretty high, due to the news that I had to move from my childhood home. James and I were getting closer and closer, and started experimenting a little bit. A kiss here, a touch there…nothing serious but enough to heighten our feelings for each other.

Moving day was approaching, my sadness and anger was growing. I wanted James to know just how much he meant to me over the last 2 years. I couldn't tell him in person, that would be too embarrassing. So, I wrote him a letter, including parts of some of our favorite songs. We loved those songs, and they were special to me because he introduced me to all these great bands. I assumed he would know the lyrics were from our songs, and that he would keep the letter forever.

Well, that was the plan…

My plan had a major flaw in it. I hadn't considered what to do if James wasn't home when I went to deliver the letter. Keep the letter until I saw James in person? Leave it in the mailbox? I mean, it had his name on it so everyone would know it was meant for him, right?

Just as I was about to put the letter in the mailbox, James' little sister came around the corner. She must have been playing in the back yard, as she didn't hear the doorbell. I asked her if James was home and she said no. I told her I wanted to give him something, a letter and without thinking of the consequences, I asked her if she would give it to him for me. I told her it was special and only meant for his eyes. I asked her if I could trust her to do that for me.

She said yes, and it turned out to be one of the biggest, farthest-reaching mistakes of my life.

I put too much faith in James' little sister, she was young, and I was naïve. I called James the next day to see if he had read the letter, but he couldn't come to the phone. I tried again a couple of times that day but never talked to him. Days later, I saw him while walking the neighbourhood. I called out to him; he stopped but didn't want to stay long. I asked him why he was acting weird.

That's when I found out what had happened.

James' little sister told his mom that I had written James a letter. Like any good parent, I suppose she wanted to read it to see if she needed to protect him from anything. At the time, I just thought she was super nosy and a busy-body, but that was the pain talking. Either way, she sure didn't like what I wrote, telling James he could no longer be my friend. I think it was because of some of the song lyrics I wrote in there, she thought I was some kind of sexual deviant wanting to take her son's innocence away. I never thought that I would get him in trouble, like I said, the thought never even entered my mind. James was mad at me too, not only did I make his parents question the hell out of him, but I caused him to lose his best friend as well, me. He told his parents the words were just lyrics from songs, but they didn't believe him.

I was such a stupid, impulsive kid, but I had a good heart and truly meant well. James came to my house a few times so we could hang out without his parents knowing. Not sure if I am lucky or not, but James' parents never told mine about the letter, I wish they had of though, because maybe we could have resolved if right then and there. Instead, James' mom felt compelled to tell everyone she knew (who had boys) to stay clear of me. She told them I was a bad kid who wanted to do sexual things...at least that is what I think she told them. Word spread among the families that had boys my age in French Immersion. It was like she felt she had to protect all the boys, who were about to enter junior high, from such a deviant as me. I didn't even know about this for over a year. I might never have found out, but a new guy, whom I really liked, told me. This was how I started junior high school.

Things got worse; a lot worse.

Chapter 16

New School, new opportunities

I remember the first day of junior high school like it was yesterday. The school was huge, it seemed as big as a football field to me. I was both excited, nervous and totally scared of getting lost. There were kids from over 6 elementary schools, coming together to make up grades 7-9 in this junior high school.

I ran into some girls I knew from elementary school. We were all feeling the same way, so we decided to walk into the school together. The first thing I heard in that school was a whistle, followed by the words 'fresh meat'. Real nice. Guess that was our welcome from a group of guys in Grade 8. We didn't really know what they meant, if they were trying to be funny, mean or cute.

The new grade 7 kids were sent to the cafeteria; there we found out which teacher we had for homeroom, and where to find our class. I was relieved that Samantha wasn't in my class – the school was so big, there were 3 French Immersion grade 7 classes, and lots of new people to be friends with. At least that's what I hoped. The French Immersion classes were balanced, to ensure everyone could find a few familiar faces from their elementary school. Otherwise, we were all new to each other.

James was in my class, so that was pretty nice. He started teasing me again, sometimes meanly, but he did it to a lot of girls. I guess all those new, pretty faces put him in overdrive. He wasn't alone, though, people got weird in junior high - hormonal, mean, competitive, possessive and, dare I say, horny.

Some kids looked lanky, just coming off growth spurts. Others, it seemed, would never get taller. Boobs were a hot topic in junior high - some girls had just started growing nubs, others seemed fully developed. The boys gave the girls with big boobs the most attention - if you asked the girls if they liked that, I think they'd have said 'no'! The boys didn't seem to know, or care, if they were nice, smart, funny or sweet. There were a few idiots who thought it was funny to 'snap' girls bras, or even try to undo them. I socked one guy when he did that to me in gym class – my (just starting to grow) boobs already hurt all the time. I don't think guys had any idea how painful that could be.

Like I said, idiots.

Speaking of idiots and gym class, something happened in that class that I would end up regretting to this day. The 'incidents', along with having suffered the consequences of wanting (innocently) to take off my shirt with the boys in Grade 2, made me aware that showing certain parts of your body was inappropriate, especially for girls. Our gym was huge, so several classes would occupy the gym at the same time. Consequently, several classes would also occupy the locker rooms at the same time and, we would change clothes before and after class. One day a number of girls were in the locker room, changing out of their sweaty gym clothes. Most of the French Immersion girls, like me, turned away from each other to change their shirts and bras or they went into the bathroom stalls to change. One of the girls, though, didn't seem to care. She changed openly and freely, as if it was the most natural thing in the world. I was shocked, and to be honest a little envious of her attitude. As these thoughts swirled around my still-shocked mind, I guess I was looking a little too long. She began to shout, "What are you looking at?"

Then she asked me if I was a 'dyke'.

I didn't know what that term meant, and I didn't understand why she was so angry. All I knew was that I wanted her to stop – everyone was looking at us, and I was super-embarrassed. I told her I wasn't looking at anything, which somehow made things worse – implying there was nothing to look at. I couldn't win. A girl named Holly stepped in to help settle things, saying that I didn't mean anything by it. God love her, she knew that I just wanted to crawl into a small hole and die. No-go – the girl just yelled at Holly and went back to me. I tried to ignore her and went on getting changed as quickly as I could. This seemed to anger the girl even further; she felt she had her claws in me, and she wasn't about to let go, "Don't ignore me, I'm talking to you".

I couldn't wait to get out of there, what a bitch - I later found out her name was Clarissa, and that she was the kind of person to stay away from. I didn't wait around to hear what more she had to say, except her parting shot, "See you around". Ominous... because although the school was big, it didn't seem hard to find people if you wanted to.

That was the beginning of me getting bullied with a capital "B".

Chapter 17

Three New People Come Into Play

Bullying didn't happen every day but the more times it occurred and the more people that bullied me, the greater the lasting effect and the quieter and darker I became. James and I continued to be friends, but it was never the same as when we lived close to each other.

There were three new people I need to bring into this story. One is the boy I had a crush on for 3 years. He was the ideal guy, the handsome, dark haired guy with eyes so blue you could get lost in them. He was super nice, happy and innocent; you could tell he hadn't seen or experienced much bad in his life, at least at that time. He also seemed to be within my reach, but thanks to James' mom he was kind of scared of me and we never fully came to be. We lost touch after junior high school so I can't say whether he experienced bad things later or not. He was like a beacon of light for me during those years, the one that showed me there were still good people out there. His name was Quinn.

I had never met the second person before, she showed up in Grade 8, having moved from out west. She wasn't in my class, but everyone was talking about her, especially the boys. She had long, pretty blonde hair, big lips, big boobs and crystal blue eyes. She was of slim build and had a laugh that was sweet and infectious. Her name was Jane.

The third person, who played a pivotal role in my junior high school years, was Rochelle. I met her at a summer camp, just before middle school. We actually didn't get along at all at the summer camp. I thought she was annoying and whiny, and who knows what she first thought of me. Either way, we were snotty to each other. When we re-met in junior high, somehow, we became good friends. When we hung out, it was mostly just the two of us, and I sometimes found it hard to relate with her because she was not sporty like me. I still had peripheral friends from elementary school, and I wanted to be part of their group - hanging out at lunch time. I tried to bring Rochelle into the larger group a couple of times, but she never seemed comfortable and preferred we hang out alone. This made it more and more difficult to relate to Rochelle. We stayed friends for a year, maybe less...

I still wanted a big friend group, full of happy people who were nice and just wanted to have fun and I was ready to make real friends with more people. One day, I got my chance. Similar to Samantha, Nancy was one of the most popular French Immersion students in school. I assume she was that way in elementary school too. She was not a beauty queen, had a slight built and had a bit of extra weight around the middle. Nancy's parents did well for themselves, they had a big house in an ideal spot close to the school. Everyone from the area knew who she was and were friends with her or at least it seemed that way. She also liked basketball, like me.

Nancy was in my homeroom class in Grade 8 and so was Rochelle. One day as the class was lining up to leave the room, Nancy told me to come up the line and stand with her. I was curious what she wanted and so I left my spot with Rochelle and went to see what

Nancy wanted. Rochelle protested and I soon found out why. I got in line with Nancy, and she said she thought I was nice and wanted to be friends, then she asked me why I was hanging out with someone like Rochelle. I didn't understand so I said, "Why not"? Nancy proceeded to say some things that were not very nice about Rochelle, including that she was a loser and had no friends. She basically told me that if I wanted to be part of the "in crowd" she would bring me in, but I had to dump Rochelle first.

During this whole conversation, Rochelle was getting more and more agitated and kept asking me to come back to where she was. I kept telling her, "In a minute", but I never went back. I was so desperate to make more friends, to laugh and to have fun. I tried to get Nancy to allow Rochelle to come into the group too, but there was no way. She said that if I stayed with Rochelle, it would hold me back, and that I would be a loser too. Those were incredibly compelling words for someone like me. I regret the way I did it, but I dropped Rochelle as a friend. I basically stopped talking to her cold, and that was cold. I know I had my own mind, and I could have told Nancy to screw herself, but I didn't. I felt like I had to do this, or I would be shunned by everyone, just like Samatha tried to do to me in the 6th grade. I wanted to fit in so badly, that I justified dumping Rochelle as a friend by telling myself that I had not been relating to Rochelle lately, and this was my chance to have a big group of friends.

And I did have a big group of friends, for a while...

What I didn't know at the time was the influence I had over Rochelle. I thought she was ok; she found another friend or two. She gave me dirty looks in the hall, which I couldn't blame her for. She made friends that were socially more similar to her, friends that could give her more than I could, and I was happy for her. All the while, she was harboring resentment. She was waiting, watching for the moment that she could hurt me back, hurt me in a much bigger way.

In the next year, she got her chance. We 'll get to that later.

Chapter 18

Red, Green or Yellow

With me being ADHD, I didn't normally think things through before I made a decision, or before I acted on something. Those things, as you may recall, got me in trouble, both figuratively and literally.

There was this thing that went around the school – no idea who started it. One day some guy came up to me and asked, "Are you green, yellow or red?" I had no idea what he meant. He said, "Red means you'll do anything. Green means you won't do anything, and yellow is somewhere in the middle." Being (still) a bit naïve, I assumed he meant activity-wise, like sports, or bungy-jumping, or trying new foods. With this in mind, I told him I was 'red', up for anything. Understandably, he walked away with a smile on his face. Also understandably, I never thought about it again.

Until, of course, I found out what it meant.

Three things happened because of the red category associated with me:

The boys in French Immersion were further convinced of what James's mother had told their parents.

More boys were showing interest in me, especially the English boys, and those in higher grades.

The mean girls, the bullies, now had even more reason to bully me, because the English boys were 'theirs'.

AARRGGHHH, I just couldn't get anything right.

Shortly after I labelled myself 'red', our school had one of their monthly dances. Boys I did not know were asking me to slowdance, which was flattering, so of course I said yes. One Grade 9 boy grossed me out, while we were dancing, he was rubbing my back and rubbing up against me. I felt something odd, which I first assumed was his hand. It wasn't shaped like a hand, though, and it didn't really move like a hand.

It was his dick.

I was totally grossed out and immediately pulled away. Not really reading the moment, he asked if I would be his girlfriend. When he didn't get the answer he wanted, he got mad and called me a 'tease' – another term with which I would become familiar. Confusing days...

Starting to feel like things could be connected, I started asking around to understand what the red, green and yellow categories meant, and what a 'tease' was. I was shocked and upset when I found out what they really meant. Red meant that you would do anything sexual, including having sex. Green meant that you would do nothing sexual, probably because you were too scared or young. Yellow meant that you would do some sexual things, but not all.

And it was all recorded in 'the book'.

I had tried to be cool, and say I was 'red'. If I had known what the colors were all about, I never would have said red. I found the guy who first asked me about the colours and tried to get him to change my colour - he said he wasn't in charge of the book. The book? It all came clear in that moment. The boys came up with a rating system, and recorded it all in a book, so they'd know who they could score with. What a bunch of pigs. With the exception of the 'incidents', I had next to no sexual experience. But according to the book...

The boys in French Immersion didn't seem interested in dating me. I found it curious that the whole group would shun me. I asked Quinn about it, which is when I found out what James' mother had done. Apparently, our own church was the gossip hot-spot, and James' mother had found herself 'preaching' the bad news on numerous occasions. And word spread fast.

I really hadn't done anything, but half the people in my world believed I was a 'slut'.

Boys in my grade were afraid I might defile them, and the girls were avoiding becoming a 'slut' by association. I figured at that point; my dating pool was reduced to the English boys – who knew only of my 'red' status. Even that backfired on me, as the boys I dated soon realized I was not the 'red' they had hoped for.

Even those brief relationships with English boys raised the ire of the mean girls. Could I help it if the boys were interested in me and not them? No, but I was easy to blame. It started with bathroom wall graffiti. This artwork ranged from innocent 'Beth + Corey' love declarations, to specific, targeted and disparaging tags. The messages about me were getting more frequent, and meaner.

Karen is a slut.

There it was, in black and white. Or etched into blue bathroom stall paint, at least. I sat there peeing, looked at the wall, and my world changed. I was devasted, hurt and embarrassed. It wouldn't matter if it was true or not, all the girls in the school were going to end up seeing it. Why was I so hated by some? I wondered who carved those words into the walls of the stall. There were a few 'usual suspects', but in reality, it could have been any girl in the school.

Today I believe "It gets better", but at the time, things only got worse. Chatter, dirty looks and random calls of 'slut' in the hallways – reminiscent of that song *Highschool Confidential*. It was constant. One day, while driving in the car with my parents, I glanced up at one of the grey, cement walls supporting an overpass. There was a lot of graffiti, but one short statement jumped out at me.

Karen is a slut. I knew it was for me because my last name was there too.

Mortified, pissed and embarrassed... the mean girls had gone too far. Those bitches, unwilling to restrict their bullying to the school, wanted the whole town to know the rumors as well. I quickly looked to see if my parents had noticed, fortunately they had their eyes fixed on the road ahead. It was of little comfort though, as we had a lot of family in town. Uncles, aunts, cousins... all driving past graffiti about me - I felt helpless, I didn't know where they even got spray paint, and I didn't want to bring attention to the fact that someone is spray painting things about me in the city. So, I said nothing, and kept all my sadness and anxiety inside.

My friendship with Nancy didn't last long. She wasn't mean to me, but she was mean. Having been bullied, I guess I grew more sensitive to gossip and rumors, even if they were about someone else. She was a small-b bully, but I couldn't be friends with anyone who bullied anyone, to any degree. I distanced myself from her, hanging out with people I had known for a long time, or with Quinn. Having a pool helped, as I'd invite a few friends for a lunchtime swim when the days got warmer.

Almost every day, I was told that someone wanted to beat me up. Some of them I knew, some I didn't. It was really fun going to school wondering who was watching for me, wondering if they would catch me in an enclosed space, like the washroom or a locker room. I often wondered what I would do if I found myself in that situation - I had never been in a fight, I didn't know how to throw a punch or how to block one. I even asked my parents if they could put me in karate class – aside from the punches and kicks, it would have helped my confidence in dealing with difficult situations. They asked me why, but I didn't want to tell them the real reason. Without any justification for the class, and remembering when I quit gymnastics, they probably thought I would just waste their money, so they said no. That was my fault for not telling them the real reason.

Looking back, the thought of getting into a fight was probably much worse than an actual fight would have been.

One day at school, like most days, a 'messenger' told me that some girl wanted to fight me.

At that point, I had had it with everything – the graffiti, the bullying, rumors, colours… it was just all too much. Even though I didn't know who this girl was, I said, "Yeah, why not, I'll fight her". The messenger ran back inside, and that was it. I heard nothing more that day and was starting to question if it was a real threat or not. That question was answered at the end of the day, as I heard someone yelling my name. Her name was Nina.

"Ok, this is it" I thought, as a short, pretty Indigenous girl approached me outside. The indigenous kids had a reputation – they were tough, lived a rough life and they could fight. Great. The first thing she said to me, was that she heard I wanted to fight her. I said, "why would I want to fight you, I don't even know you", and I told her that someone had told me she wanted to fight me.

We soon realized we had been set up, that someone had manipulated the two of us into a confrontation. Neither Nina, nor I, wanted to fight, and I explained that it was probably Clarissa –

that she was always bugging me, and trying to get me in fights. The mention of Clarissa seemed to ignite something in Nina. She said, "I don't like Clarissa either, she's always trying to cause trouble". Was Nina a potential ally? Nina said OK, confirmed that I didn't want to fight and walked away, I was so relieved. From then on, we said hi in the hallways and were even on the school basketball team together. We weren't actually friends, but we were friendly, and it was nice to know that someone else hated Clarissa as much as I did.

Grade 8 drew to a close, and I was looking forward to a great summer. Quinn and I hung out several times that summer - we kissed a few times and held hands, but never officially said we were boyfriend and girlfriend. I can only assume that even though he liked me, the rumors James' mom spread probably held him back from wanting to be my boyfriend. He did actually take me to his house a few times, but he probably didn't tell his parents who I was.

One of the big things in junior high school was listening to the radio at night and dedicating songs to each other on the local pop/rock radio channel once a week. It was a special program for all the lovebirds, and you had one hour to get your song and dedication in. It was fun, the radio guy would say whatever you wanted...within reason of course. I feel passionately in love with some of the songs the rock bands sang, I swear the late 80's produced some of the best love songs ever, songs like:

I'll Be There for You by Bon Jovi
When I Look into Your Eyes by Firehouse
Don't Cry by Guns and Roses
Every Rose Has It's Thorn by Poison

There were so many amazing songs I just can't list them all, but you should look them up. When I would hear those songs, my passion ignited, and I would sing my ass off. I mostly dedicated songs to Quinn when that radio show was on, but I also dedicated some songs to a couple of other boys during my junior high school years that I had been dating at the time.

Near the end of summer, my parents put me in a church camp for a week. It may have had something to do with an assignment in Grade 8. It was an independent project, and we could choose any topic to research and write about. I tend to work better within parameters, preferring assignments with clear, articulated instructions over 'free reign'. I also tended to procrastinate, so when it got down to the wire, I chose my topic.

I was going to research the devil.

My plan was to compare my research on the devil with what I was taught in Sunday School. As you may remember, I stopped believing in God after the 'incidents'. My mother was upset when she discovered the subject of my project. Concerned I was going to become a Satan-worshiper, she contacted my teacher. Needless to say, I didn't end up doing my project on Satan. If memory serves, I don't think I did the project at all – they exempted me, likely thinking I had a real problem. Understandably, it was difficult for people to accept that it was just innocent research... a legitimate academic pursuit, whatever.

People believe what they want to believe. I learned that a long time ago.

I don't know if it was my teacher, or someone else, who told my mom about 'church camp'. My parents were obviously looking for some kind of help with me. They felt I needed to be in more wholesome surroundings, in hopes they would help bring me out of whatever had been getting me down. I had gone to similar camps before, so I didn't put much of a fuss up when my parents told me I was going. When we got close to the location, it was quite peaceful and beautiful. The dirt road into the camp was far off the main road and it seemed to take forever to get there. Big trees lined the dirt road into the camp and seemed to stretch up for miles. You could smell the fresh air which had a hint of pine coming off the large trees. I couldn't even get my arms around some of the trees. The first building I saw was the large wooden lodge, it looked well taken care of and was very inviting. We were warmly greeted by the church minister and the main camp organizer. They told me there would soon be an orientation meeting and told me which cabin I was in so I could meet the girls in my cabin along with the cabin counselor. I said goodbye to my parents and approached my assigned cabin. While approaching the cabin, I could see other cabins surrounding the lake. I was happy to see the water and was looking forward to a swim.

I was nervous walking towards my cabin wondering if I would like the girls in my cabin and if they would like me. A week is a long time to spend in a place if you didn't like the people around you and if they didn't like you either. I held my breath and opened the cabin door. I was very surprised to see several girls whom I knew. Of all people, Jane was there so I was super excited though I didn't show it because I wanted to look cool. We looked at each other in shock, not expecting to know anyone. Not only did I know Jane but there were 3 other girls I knew or recognized from junior high school. The other ones were Amy, whom I had known and have been in classes with since Grade 1, and Stephanie, who was in English, but I recognized. The last girl I also knew, and was concerned about as it was Rochelle. Yes, Rochelle, the same former friend that I had dropped the year before. Seeing her gave me anxiety because I was worried, she would tell the other girls that I was an awful person and couldn't be trusted. To my surprise however, she kept silent about that and after a day or two I relaxed, and we all had a great time.

The main lodge was huge and served both as our dining area, as well as a gathering area where we would listen to daily sermons and learn what God had to offer us.

The five of us became close really fast. Guess that happens when you spend 24/7 with each other for a week. We talked about a lot of stuff, including our families and how we grew up. I didn't tell them about the bullying, I was worried they would think I was a loser. We swam in the lake on every hot day even though it was a bit cold, we also checked out the boys that were there and we laughed, a lot.

There was something else that some of us had in common too. During the one hour of daily sermon, the minister kept talking about how God loves us, no matter what we've done. That made me cry because I didn't believe I deserved to be loved, whether God existed or not. So many bad things had happened to me, and I was a bad kid, at least all the adults thought so. Within the first few days, I could no longer sit and listen to the sermons - I had to get out of there. I felt I didn't deserve to be in that place of God, and that made my skin crawl. I wasn't the only one who felt that way, both Jane and Amy seemed to share the same feeling because they rose after I did and left as well. We left with tears in our eyes and talked about feeling undeserving, though I didn't share the real reasons I felt that way. I respected the Minister and the camp organizer because they did not force us to come back to the sermons, they talked to us daily though and told us that we were always welcome. Personally, I just couldn't participate in that part of the camp. For the rest of the week, the three of us just walked and talked or stayed in our cabin during that part of the day.

By the end of the week, it felt like the 5 of us girls were thick as thieves, but I didn't want to assume that we would still be friends when school started back up.

Chapter 19

New Friendships That Soon Ended

When Grade 9 came around, Quinn and I were still hanging out a bit. We decided early in the year that no matter who we were dating, we would go to prom together. I couldn't be happier. He was my knight in shining armor, my perfect potential. As I mentioned before, he was the light for me, the only consistent and pure thing I had.

I really hoped that both Quinn and Jane would be in my homeroom class, but neither were. James was in my class, as was Rochelle. Jane's class turned out to be just down the hall, where I saw the girls from church camp chatting together. I wanted to approach, to see if they still wanted to be friends, though I was wary. I had such a good time with them at camp that I had to see if those friendships could continue. To my surprise, Jane seemed as excited to see me as I was to see her. When they started to leave to go outside, she asked if I was coming - I was so happy, I didn't hesitate to join them. So far, so good.

I always held the fear that Rochelle would turn on me like I had done to her, but she seemed fine, and we got along well, so I let my guard down and we were comfortable around each other, we were friends just like the rest of the group. I did apologize to her for dumping her back then and told her I shouldn't have. I told her Nancy, and I were not friends for long and that I couldn't stand how she was always talking about people behind their backs. Rochelle said she could have told me that about Nancy. Regardless, I told her I made a mistake and that I was happy to be friends again. She said the same and we hugged. I never questioned or checked in on that with her again. I trusted her and so believed all was well.

Although Jane was not in my class, she just lived down the street from me - it was super-easy for us to get together. All the girls from church camp started hanging out in school and outside of school. I felt on top of the world, like I was invincible. We were all similar in height and body shape, except Jane had the largest chest and Stephanie was an inch or two taller than the rest of us. We all had shoulder length hair, four blondes and one brunette – me, the dark horse, the black sheep. It wasn't just the hair that made me stand out - I had a skin tone that always seemed tanned, especially when I was right beside them.

We were inseparable for about 5 months, all hanging out together at school and at each other's houses. There weren't many times that we split up, because we had more fun together. We went to some parties; did things we shouldn't really do and laughed a lot together. The bullying seemed to slow by Clarissa and her friends too, maybe because there was strength in numbers. Or maybe because our group was made up of English and French Immersion girls. It's also possible that because Jane was well liked by everyone, they thought Karen can't be that bad if she is friends with Jane. I'll never know. What I did know was that I felt stronger, more liked, more powerful - everyone knew our group, people would move out of the way for us when we walked down the hall, and there was always someone saying hi. It felt good. It felt really good. I was still scared to get caught alone in the bathroom with one of my bullies, but there was no more hiding at lunchtime, no more worries of being beaten up. It's like I was in a gang of beautiful girls and people had some kind of respect for us.

I started to be invited to different places because of the group I was in, places like the 'front path'. As it sounds, the front path was a path at the front of the school – but it was so much more than that. It was close enough to the school, but far enough away that the teachers never went there. It was the place where the 'cool girls' and 'tough girls' hung out, and the place I tried my first cigarette – something I thought I'd sort of pick-up to fit in.

There was an indigenous girl who hung out at the front path, and she did not like me. She had heard all the rumors about me, and how even though we were friends again now, I had dumped Rochelle as a friend the year before. She was several inches taller than any of us, with dark eyes and long, straight black hair. Her name was Sally. I didn't bother explaining or justifying my actions in the past to her, I simply told her which parts were true and which weren't. No matter how many times we hung out, Sally never liked me, she either didn't trust me or was jealous...not sure.

I always say that I was never addicted to cigarettes, an argument I hold to this day. I never smoked at home, only a few times during the school-week, and occasionally on weekends if I was out and there were some around. Back then I never bought a pack either, just bummed a drag here and there and, on a few occasions, a whole one, but even then, someone would ask you for a drag anyway, so it was never like you had one completely to yourself.

Rochelle also lived near me but wasn't as close to my house as Jane's house was. Rochelle's house was probably 4x as far as Jane's house was to me. Even though we usually all hung out together, sometimes we would hang out one on one. One day, when Rochelle and I were roaming the streets around her house, she had a cigarette and some matches, so we sparked it up and started to share it. Whenever I took a drag in public, I was always worried that someone would see me smoking and tell my parents – I was on high-alert. Well wouldn't you know it, as Rochelle and I walked (and smoked) around the neighborhood towards my house, my parents drove up behind us. We were in the middle of the street, and I had the cigarette in my hand at the time. Thankfully, I saw them before they realized it was us and I whipped the cigarette onto the road. They hadn't seen us smoking it, but they slowed down the car and stopped to talk to us... I was freaking out inside and I started to notice the smoke from the smouldering cigarette rise in the air. I thought if I don't stamp this out my parents are going to see it and I won't be able to get out of this one. Much to Rochelle's annoyance I stepped on it and turned my heel to put the cigarette out. My parents soon said goodbye and Rochelle went to see if the cigarette could be salvaged, it couldn't be. I had made sure of that, and she was pissed. She said it was hard to get, and that she had taken it from her mom. All I could do was say sorry, and I asked her if she would have rather my parents found out and possibly tell her parents too? She said, "No" and that was that. Man, I nearly shit my pants though.

Not sure why but there always seemed to be some kind of drama in our girl gang. You couldn't usually see it from the outside, but there were frequent little tiffs. Rochelle and Stephanie were frequently snotty with each other, as were Amy and Jane. Where did I sit? I was always on the sidelines; I was never outwardly mean to any of them like they were to each other. Having been bullied as much as I was, this kind of conflict made me uncomfortable. I would ignore it when they were at each other about something, and I never said much about it. I didn't like it though, I wish it didn't happen because I really liked all of them, and I couldn't understand why they irked each other so much.

It was probably just puberty.

The first time I went to Jane's house, I was in for quite a surprise. At school, Jane always seemed happy, and she laughed a lot. You can imagine my surprise, then, when I got to Jane's house and saw how she treated her parents. They said hi to us, to which I responded, but Jane just ignored them. They asked her, "Who's your friend?", which was also ignored. When, "We're talking to you!" followed, Jane lost it. She yelled at them to shut up and to leave her alone. Holy shit - I had never heard anyone talk to their parents like that. I was completely shocked and didn't know what to say.

Jane's parents sensed my discomfort and asked me if I ever spoke to my parents that way. When I answered no, they asked me why not. "Cause my dad would probably kick my butt" was all I could think of. Jane's parents said she could learn a lot from me, which really set her off. After telling them to 'fuck off', she stormed up to her room, with me in tow. I was flabbergasted - I asked her why she was so mad at her parents; did she hate them? She said she didn't hate them, she just always talked to them that way. It made me uncomfortable every time I was there – it made me squirm inside. I just couldn't imagine talking to my parents that way.

During lunch hours, we would sometimes buy a bag of chips then hang out at the front path. Other times, we would go to my house for lunch because it was the closest. Whenever we went to my house, we always left a mess. There just wasn't enough time to clean up, so we'd leave all the dishes on the counter. When my mom would get home from work, that would be the first thing she'd see. Upset by this, my mom asked if we could, as a group, go to Jane's house once in a while, just to give her a break. I must admit, I thought it would be nice to switch it up too.

Jane had no interest in that.

She said going all the way to her house would cut into our lunch-hour too much. I am not sure if it was hormones, or the influence of my parents, but I started to look at the situation differently. Was it possible the girls were just using me? They never thought to clean up after themselves, or offered to help me clean up their mess. I felt like my whole noon hour was spent catering to them, and they seemed to be taking me for granted. I would get one a glass of water, put the water away and sit down, then another would ask for water. It was so annoying, and after a while I started to wonder if they were doing it on purpose. I tried to be nice, but having been bullied in the past, and with the whispers of my mother in my ear, I just came to believe they were using me. One day I was really quiet, stewing, and every time someone asked me for something I glared at them. They were like "whoa, I just asked for a drink of water" and I knew they were right, but I also couldn't seem to stop myself from being angry.

If Rochelle still had some ill feelings for me regarding the past and if she was waiting for an opportunity to get back at me, this was the opening she could have been waiting for. I say this because I don't know if she had a plan to get back at me or if the situation just presented itself.

But…

The next day, I found the girls by the lockers as the lunch-bell rang. They said they were going to Jane's house for lunch; I asked if I could come with them. Jane said we could all be together, but only if we went to my house and if I was nice. Wanting to be sure, or hoping I had heard it wrong, I asked them, "Are you saying, the only way I can be with you is if we go to my house?" The answer was yes. I was so hurt, so mad… I argued that I was getting in trouble every day for the state we would leave my house in. "Can't we just go to your house sometimes, Jane?" The answer was no.

There it was, I was in the group if they could use my house on lunch-hours, otherwise, I was out.

I know they had been discussing my attitude, and I don't blame them, but I also think they were being unfair. I assume, but will never know, that Rochelle innocently mentioned my attitude and that maybe they shouldn't be friends with me anymore. I have no doubt that she delighted in the idea of me getting dumped, the way I had dumped her the previous year. Maybe she didn't mean for it to last, maybe she thought she would just teach me a lesson and then in a few days we'd all be friends again, but it didn't go that way, it didn't go that way at all.

I felt lost, I really did, like I was falling into a black hole and would never see the light of day. I was so sad, and had no idea who I would, or even could be friends with. Rochelle got her wish (if that was what she wanted) – I now knew what it felt like to be dumped as a friend. It felt terrible, I didn't know what to do, I thought I had something special and now I had nothing. There was a lot of awkward explaining to acquaintances who wondered what happened between us girls – everyone else thought we were inseparable. And the bullies did what bullies do – they pounced on the vulnerable one cut loose from the herd.

Sheepishly, I returned to a previous group of friends, walking the school grounds during lunch. Quinn was usually there, which helped. It was nice, but it wasn't the same - I never felt as close to them. Maybe there wasn't enough time left in the school year, or maybe I was closed off from letting anyone in too much. I don't think any of them knew I was bullied, aside from the graffiti in the girl's washroom and the occasional insult in the halls. As much as I didn't like the way they behaved sometimes, I missed my former best friends. I missed them dearly, and I never felt more alone than when they walked by as a group, laughing and carrying on. It was like one of those teen movies when the popular girls would walk down the hall in slow-motion, flipping their hair, sneering at the lesser-than's.

I was invisible to them, and part of me grew even darker inside.

Even though I had some friendships, some reasons to be happy, I started to obsess about my own funeral. Would anyone show up? Would my classmates? Jane? Quinn? I probably thought about that once or twice a week. Sometimes, while in the bath, I would look at my hairdryer on the counter and wonder… Would it hurt? Would it work? Just drop it, plugged in, right in the bath with me… Could I, do it? Would I?

Rochelle treated me the worst because we were still in the same class. She would take any opportunity to tell the teacher on me, or make fun of me while getting others to join in. It didn't always work but it sure made me want to hurt her, I wanted something bad to happen to her. I also wanted the same fate for Clarissa. I can understand how some victims take revenge on their bullies, hurting them in ways they would never expect. I think bullies see their victims as weak, spineless. That's likely how they pick their targets anyway, someone they can have power over.

After my breakup with the girl friends, not everything went bad – I still had a boyfriend, named Charlie, at least for a time. He had been going out for 4 months. He had long dark, straight hair and cool cloudy blue-grey eyes. He was in English. I called him one day, and I was sure I'd heard another voice in his room. It was a girl's voice, and it turned out to be Jane. I felt hurt, betrayed… I assumed they liked each other, why else would they be together in his room? I confronted them, they said it was innocent. There was no way I could believe them, not after everything that happened.

Apparently, Jane was having trouble at home. At the end of that school day, she was out front by the busses, talking to my boyfriend. Jane said she couldn't go home, so he invited her to his house – that was supposedly what happened. Seemed fishy to me, so Charlie and I soon ended it. He thought I was too jealous, and I thought he was too into Jane – regardless of how she felt about him.

Now I had no boyfriend, and no girlfriends.

Though it wouldn't have seemed possible, this made me even more vulnerable to the bullying of Clarissa and her friends. It started with taunting me about not being friends with Jane and the girls, and not having Charlie anymore. Since Charlie was in English with them, I am sure that us breaking up further delighted Clarissa and her friends. I didn't think I could possibly feel worse, then I did.

And I started to feel scared all the time.

Chapter 20 Me and my fam

You may have noticed I haven't mentioned my family much so far. There are reasons for that, but I'll give you a bit about them now. From childhood through the end of university, I wasn't really close to my immediate family. I was a burden right from the start for my parents, but especially my mom. My dad worked two jobs, and didn't seem to spend much of his spare time around us. He was the authority in the house though, making final decisions on most things, like what I was and wasn't allowed to do. When I got hurt, like when I fell off my bike and skinned my knees, he was the one I ran to, the one I wanted caring for me. Not unlike me, he loved swimming - in his youth he was part of the Fredericton diving team.

When he wasn't working, it wasn't hard to get him to take me to the pool, and I always wanted to go to the pool.

My mom got the raw end of the deal, always having to deal with my crap - either at school or at home. It wasn't all bad, but it was probably chaotic most of the time - no doubt I exhausted her. With my dad not being around a lot, I think she resented her situation – blaming him, or me, or most likely both of us. Either way, it was me she was yelling at. As I got older, I got more defiant. Things got worse, and I kept more and more from my family.

I also mentioned that I had a sister, Hannah, she was 18 months older than me. She was pretty, with long blond wavy hair and blue eyes. Not only was I her annoying little sister, but I was also the problem child, taking our mom's attention away, which I can imagine led my sister to resent me as well. I remember we were almost the same height in junior high school. I may have been slightly smaller than her, but we could fit in the same clothes. My sister used to go into my room to borrow clothes, but when I did the same to her it was an issue. She liked wearing my clothes, but it was not a two-way street.

I recall the first week of junior high school, when her friends met me. They couldn't believe how much we looked alike, aside from the hair and skin tones, and how much we sounded alike. Her friends thought that was cool, but she did not share their perception. In fact, I think it bugged the shit out of her.

We only had one phone line when we were growing up, a land line. She would get so annoyed when I was on the phone if she needed it. Just like the clothes deal, it was not an even trade. If I was using the phone when she wanted it, I was to get off immediately, and if I didn't, she yelled at me and told my mom. When the roles were reversed, she'd ignore me – staying on for another hour at times.

I never felt like I had a great relationship with any of my immediate family, so I wasn't inclined to talk about my problems with them - friend problems, boy problems, bullying problems... I kept them all to myself. Even when they knew there were problems, like the breakup with Jane and the girls, it just wasn't discussed.

I put it on myself to figure it all out on my own.

Chapter 21

The Baddest Guy In School

Even though my junior high school was big, there were some people all the kids knew. Jesse was the baddest guy in school. He had light brown hockey hair and for those of you not from Canada, hockey hair means short in the front and long in the back. This hairstyle had different names depending on where you are from and here are a few examples: Mullet, Camaro Hair, Beaver Paddle, Business in the Front, Party in the Back. There are certainly others but too many to list here. So, he had hockey hair, he was close to 6 ft. tall, had a wide back, light brown eyes and a built body. He wasn't the hottest guy around, but he was pleasant enough to look at. I thought Jane and Jesse were a couple once, but I guess they were just friends. She had dated his cousin for a short while, maybe that's why she didn't or wouldn't date Jesse, but I still think Jesse had a thing for her.

One day, an acquaintance told me that Jesse liked me and wanted to be my boyfriend. Although I was a bit nervous because of his reputation, I thought, "why not?" – I had nothing else going for me. Maybe life would get more exciting. First though, I had to make sure that Jane was ok with it because as I said, I thought they hung out or dated and I didn't want to do anything to make her like me even less.

Jesse assured me all was well with Jane, and that we were ok to be boyfriend and girlfriend. I didn't tell my parents for a month or more though, because they had judged kids in the past based on their last names and since I knew Jesse's family was pretty rough, I knew they would recognize his last name and judge him before they even met him. When the time came, that's exactly what they did. By then, though, I didn't care. I thought I was in love.

Despite rumours of Jesse having a temper and getting in lots of fights, he was really quite sweet to me. He wanted people to know I was his girlfriend, and when I was around him, I felt safe. Safe from my bullies anyway. He even told Clarissa and her friends to leave me alone, and they actually did what he said. In a way, he saved me for a while, and for that I guess I will always be grateful. He was powerful, in that people were afraid of him and listened to him, and he was good to me.

I knew that being with someone like him was going to lead me to go further than I ever had with anybody else. Even though I wasn't really ready to have sex, I know he would expect it and if I wanted to stay with him and have his safety, I would have to do it eventually. Eventually arrived, and I let him do what he wanted. I probably would have done anything to keep my school days bully free, and to no longer be scared all the time. I still didn't want to end up alone with one of my bullies in the hall, in the bathrooms or outside with them alone but the fear of them jumping me dissipated somewhat.

I wanted to check with Jane first, to see if she would be upset if Jesse and I did it. I still wasn't 100% convinced that she had no feelings for him. We called her from his house, she said she didn't care what we did. I felt a bit like he was rubbing it in her face, but I didn't focus on that much

After the phone call we went upstairs to his bedroom, and it happened. I didn't think having sex with him was all that special, but what did I have to compare it to...nothing. I wish Jane had put up a fuss about it or told me not to do it with him. Since we weren't friends anymore, I had no guidance from girlfriends. I didn't want to be alone and decided to do whatever was necessary to prevent that. My life was chaos, but I could control this. I decided when I would lose that precious thing, some don't get the chance to decide but I did. I decided for myself - who, what, when and where. It was good for a few months.

He told me he loved me. I thought I loved him too.

After a while, I started to get tired of the number of fights he was getting in. He seemed to get in a fight at least once a week, and most often I learned of it from someone else – not from him. I thought it was stupid and I saw no reason for it. I think you can see why I started to doubt being with Jesse. I was bullied a lot, and I just couldn't respect being with someone that was beating up other guys on a pretty consistent basis, I couldn't stand behind that kind of behavior. He had told me more than once that he didn't want people to think he was a bad guy and that he didn't want the reputation his last name brought, well then why was he always fighting someone? I remember asking him why he got in so many fights and his reasons were pretty dumb, so and so said they wanted to fight, or I don't like that person. That made no sense to me, what was he trying to prove?

I stayed with Jesse for a few more months. He and Jane continued to be friends, and they were supposed to go to prom together. I had no problem with that because Quinn and I had made that promise to go to prom with each other no matter who we were dating. You know, I don't think Quinn ever actually had a girlfriend throughout junior high school. I was the closest thing he had to a girlfriend, the few times we hung out and kissed.

It was getting close to the end of the school year and because Jesse got into so many fights on and off school grounds, he was told by the principal that he was no longer permitted to go to the end of year dance – aka the prom. I felt bad for Jane, but was happy I had promised Quinn that we would go together.

Chapter 22

The Betrayal

It was getting warmer out and there were a couple of months left of junior high school for me. I am not sure if it was because of Jesse, but Jane and a larger group of her friends seemed willing to let me back in, but I had to do one thing first.

It took me awhile to decide whether I would do what they asked me to do. If you recall, I had mentioned that I had heard rumours that Gwen had been throwing parties. I guess some of them were pretty wild, and there was a lot of drinking involved. I think there must have been a few things happen at some of those parties that made Gwen a target for Jane. Jane said that I had to bring Gwen to a place away from school, so she could talk to her. Jane suspected that Gwen had slept with Jesse's cousin while she was dating him. I was torn up inside and didn't know what to do. I didn't want to put Gwen in danger, but I also wanted to be accepted back into Jane's group. People were calling Gwen a slut - I had lost touch with her, so I didn't know what was true. Since I had been friends with

Jane more recently, I believed her, but I told Jane the only way I was going to bring Gwen to the chosen spot was if she promised that they wouldn't all gang up on her. Jane promised they wouldn't gang up on Gwen, so I started working on talking to Gwen again and getting her to trust me so she would hang out with me some noon hour.

The whole time I was conflicted about misleading my former best friend, conflicted that she may be getting into trouble and that she might be out of control and conflicted by wanting to have my best friends back. I assured myself that I wouldn't let it get out of hand, that I would protect Gwen if I had to. I was trying to do it all, please Jane, and protect Gwen from anything really bad happening.

But, as life teaches you, you can't have it both ways.

The day came for me to bring Gwen to the meeting place; a place far enough away from school to get in trouble but close enough that we could all get back before noon hour was over. I told Gwen that I wanted to go to the candy store with her, like we used to when I still lived near her. I also told her that I wanted to talk to her about her life the last few years, and that I missed her, which was true. She agreed to come with me. We walked down the front path, crossed through an elementary school, and down the next street to the candy store. As we approached the store, we noticed a large group of girls gathered in front of one of the houses. I must admit, I had no idea that many people were going to be there. There must have been 15 girls, at least. Gwen was scared but I kept reassuring her that I was with her, and that I would help her if needed.

The girls began to yell – calling Gwen a slut, and a bitch. I told them to get Jane, who then came out of the house and down the stairs to where we stood. I listened, watched and scanned the scene to see if I thought it might get out of hand. Jane started yelling at

Gwen, pushed her and accused her of having sex with her ex-boyfriend, while they were still together. The girls were surrounding us, jeering at us, encouraging Jane to fight Gwen. Jane started hitting Gwen, but Gwen wouldn't fight back, she just took it.

After four or five punches, I couldn't stand it anymore, so I stepped in.

I tried to bring everything down a few notches. I reminded Jane that she said she just wanted to talk to Gwen and asked her what proof she had. Sally decided she had to step in as well but not to help Gwen, and not to help me. She warned that if I didn't get out of the way, she would start hitting me. I didn't care what might happen to me anymore; I told Jane that was enough, she had made her point. I then told them Gwen was going to go, and that no one was to follow. I said no one was going to bother her again; they were finished with her.

I told Gwen to go, and she hesitated but I said I would come find her soon, so she ran towards the store. I stayed with the group for about 5 minutes, talking to Jane making her swear that was the end. I took some insults from a few people and Sally said that I couldn't be trusted and that I was not a good person. She talked about me misleading Gwen to the spot and letting that happen to her. She didn't say it because she liked Gwen, she said it to make me feel like shit and it worked. I already felt terrible, and I hated myself for putting Gwen in that situation, Sally just spoke the truth and made me feel even worse. I told her she was right and started walking away.

Once I was sure no one was going to follow me, I left the rest of them standing there. They didn't know where Gwen went, but I did. I found her at the candy store, she was worked up but not as bad as I'd anticipated. I saw the marks on her face, where Gwen had been hit a couple of times, and I felt sick. I cried and confessed to her about the real reason I brought her there. I told her I did miss her though and still wanted to be friends. I told her I wouldn't blame her if she hated me. She said I helped to save her and that she was going to eventually run into Jane and have to talk to her anyway. This way it was controlled, and I was with her. I reassured her no one in that group would bother her again or I would be right there ready to fight by her side if needed. I asked her about what Jane had said, about her having sex with her ex-boyfriend.

She told me it was not consensual. He had raped her.

I cried with her, wanting to crawl into a hole and die right then and there. I told myself I was such a dick, and that I didn't deserve Gwen's friendship, or maybe even to be alive. I had betrayed the one true best friend I ever had, and I still tear up thinking about it today. I hate how weak I was and how I would betray an old friend just to get my other friends back.

I suggested to Gwen that she take the rest of the day off and to call her dad to come get her. She called and he came. I stayed with her until her dad arrived, until she was safe with him. I couldn't leave her alone, just in case. We hugged before she left, and I told her how sorry I was, that I would never forgive myself for doing that to her. Once she was safe in the car with her dad, I made the long walk back to school, some of the girls were still at the house and yelled at me. I just kept going, nothing they could have said would have made me feel worse than I already did.

On the walk back, instead of taking responsibility for my own actions, I seriously contemplated whether I wanted to be friends with people who lied, manipulated and imposed friendship-ultimatums on me.

Chapter 23

The Phone Call

One night when I was watching a show, alone at my house in the tv room, I received a phone call, a very upsetting phone call. When I answered the phone, there was a girl's voice on the other end that I didn't recognize, she asked "Is Karen there"? I said this is her. It was weird because she started off real nice asking me how I was doing and what I was doing? Then I asked, who is this? The question was avoided. There was no caller ID back then, no way I could find the number from which the mystery girl was calling.

She quickly started to turn the mood of the phone call from nice and polite, to mean and nasty, saying she had heard I was a slut and a bitch. Now I was scared, I had another bully in my life, and I didn't even know who she was. She said, "I also heard you have no friends" and my heart stuck in my throat, I thought if she knows that I don't have much of a friend group, then she knows I don't have a group of people that would stick up for me. She also brought up my betrayal of Gwen and said, "some friend you are". Again, I asked who she was, no reply, just a steady stream of insults - piercing my eardrums, and my heart.

"No one likes you" - "You're a slut" – "You should just go away and die" and "We are going to get you when you least expect it".

I was about to hang up, she must have sensed it. "Don't hang up", she commanded, "if you do, you'll regret it". I felt like stone. I felt like I had no control over my own life. I knew I could hang up any time, but the risk of making matters worse seemed to freeze me in place. My mind swirled, old familiar thoughts crept in, "What is my purpose, if this is it then I quit". I was really getting tired of all this crap. Why was all this happening to me? She continued to tell me not to hang up and I started to get frustrated, and she could tell because I started to raise my voice.

By then, I had drawn my parents' attention, and they opened the tv room door to ask me who I was talking to. I gave them a hand gesture that indicated for them to go away, and they did, at first. I don't know if they were trying to help me or not, but my sister soon picked up the receiver from another room and said she needed the phone. She asked how long I was going to be, and I told her that I didn't know. My sister hung up.

I was starting to get mad now because I was getting pressure from my family to get off the phone and, I was being threatened if I hung up. I tried to tell the voice on the other end of the line that I had to go. She wasn't done with me yet though. She told me to watch out for her, to look for her and to be ready.

Now I was really mad I said, "how I am supposed to look out for you when I don't even know who you are"? She said, "Don't yell at me", and "you really are a little bitch, aren't you"? You know, I started to think to myself, I really don't recognize this person's voice, and a light bulb went off in my head and I realized, this isn't one of my bullies, it's someone else, someone I really don't know. One of my bullies, got one of their friends, from a different school, to call me and I couldn't believe it. Why would one of my bullies go to such lengths to worry and to scare me?

By this time, my sister came back on the phone and said she really needed to make a call, then she yelled into the phone for me to get off right now. I was pissed, not only was I going through this shit with the person on the phone who I realized I didn't know, but I was getting in trouble at home too. I could hear my sister outside the door telling my parents that I wouldn't get off the phone, so they came in again. They could see I was visibly upset and again asked who was on the phone. They said I had to get off the phone or they were going to take it away from me. Then I got scared that if my parents took the phone out of my hands, the girl on the phone might tell my parents that I was a slut and a bitch and that I had no friends, and I didn't want that to happen so I told my parents I would get off.

I had had it now. I told the girl that I had to go and was not going to get in trouble with my family because of her. She finally said OK, then warned me again to watch out for her and I said "Yup" quite shortly. She asked me why I was giving her attitude and I thought, WTF, are you stupid…Again I said, how am I supposed to look out for you if I don't know who you are then I said, "I don't think you even go to my school". She said that she did, but I was more and more confident that she was lying. I said, "if you went to my school then I would recognize your voice", she had nothing to say back to me on that. Before we hung up, she said, "see you around Karen", not ominous or anything.

Now that the call was over, and I had minute to think, I started crying uncontrollably. I kept wondering who had put this girl up to calling me, it could be Rochelle, Clarissa, who knows. What I did know is that I must truly be hated for someone to go to those lengths to upset me. I think my heart broke a little that day. A little piece broke off when I found out James's mom had warned a bunch of other moms about me, a little piece broke off when I lost my best friends, a little piece broke off when I lost my virginity to Jesse and a bigger piece broke off when I betrayed Gwen. I don't think I had many pieces left, if any…

My mom found me crying and she started to cry too, wondering what could possibly be so wrong. I told her about the phone call and said that I was being bullied a bit at school. I asked her if I could change schools and start over but there were only a few months of school left and she was worried because the other close school had a worse reputation than mine, she figured it wouldn't be any better at the other school, so that never happened. I stayed at my school wishing the days away until junior school was over.

Chapter 24 Cheating

As I mentioned before, I was losing interest in Jesse. The last straw was when he fought his own friend. I later learned the reason they fought - his friend liked me and didn't like the way Jesse was treating me.

I had made another friend earlier in the year to a girl in Grade 8, her name was Gisele and after the phone call I started spending more and more time at her house. We weren't great friends, but she was a friend that I wanted to hang out with from time to time, and she had two brothers that were really nice too. They lived in a rougher part of town, but their place was pretty cool. I started going there quite a bit. Her parents smoked in the house; first time I had encountered that. Gisele was one year younger than me, and the two brothers were just a bit older than me. Their parents had exotic pets - one was a giant snake. When I say giant, that snake was twice as long as I was tall and was as thick as my thigh.

I wasn't scared of insects or lizards or snakes - I actually thought they were really neat. One day I was at Gisele's house, and they took the snake out. They asked me if I wanted to touch it, and I said "sure". It felt so cool, smooth and scaly at the same time. Then they put it around my neck, and they thought I better sit down so that the snake wouldn't put me off balance. It wrapped around me and tickled me with its tongue.

There was another guy who lived in Gisele's house. He was older, late teens I think, with long brown hair. Gisele's parents were letting him stay there, I guess. Her mom and all the boys smoked and sometimes I would have a drag off their cigarettes. I think when people start hanging out, they want to impress each other until they know they are solidly friends. So, the kids wanted to show me something they thought was different. Besides the exotic animals, there were books in the house, very detailed sex, story books. We would gather together on one of their beds and take turns reading those books out loud to each other. It was kinda odd, I guess, the five of us teenagers huddled on one bed. I guess we figured we would be able to hear the story better the closer we were to each other. Anyway, it was like story time but with the heat turned way, way up.

I can't say that I understood a lot of the descriptions in the books, the way they were written but it was very provocative, and it wasn't hard to imagine. Pretty sure we all got 'warm' from hearing the written words. One day, when the other kids left the room and I was alone with the older boy, he asked if he could kiss me. I said yes. We had just finished reading a part of the book and were pretty amped up, and before I knew it, one thing led to another and that was that.

It was ok while I was still at the house but when I left to walk back home, I realized what I had done. I had cheated on Jesse. I felt guilty, but convinced myself that Jesse wouldn't find out because the guy was a couple of years older and didn't go to our school. I also told myself I didn't really want to be with Jesse anymore anyway. Guess I was just trying to make myself feel better.

Well Jesse did find out and quickly too, guess the guy had a big mouth. Although he was probably just trying to look cool, he wasn't thinking how telling someone about it and including my name might hurt me. Anyway, once the guy found out my boyfriend was Jesse, he was pretty scared - I don't think I realized just how bad a reputation Jesse had at the time.

As I mentioned, I was feeling guilty and I was not happy with myself at all, I started doing some negative self-talk, telling myself I was now the slut the bullies said I was. I was also scared what others might think and do; guess I just gave them more fuel to taunt me with. I was so hard on myself that when Jesse came to meet me by the path near my house to confront me, I told him he could hit me, that I deserved it and that I still loved him. Thankfully, he said he didn't want to hit me, I think I actually surprised him with that one. He said he still loved me too and we hugged.

Things weren't really the same after that though, I couldn't bring myself to go back to that house because I was ashamed and mad at myself, and I distanced myself from Jesse too. I found out later on that Jesse had been having sex with other girls while being with me. Maybe that's why he wasn't that hard on me. I guess I wasn't that special to him after all.

Chapter 25

The Invite Back To The Group

I was worried what Jane would think, too. Out of all of them, she was the one I missed the most, and sort of wished we were still friends. My betrayal of Gwen was supposed to get me back in with them but like I said, I was debating whether I truly wanted that and neither myself nor the group were making a first move until Rochelle called me one night.

I was surprised by her call, but I guess it made sense. If she was the one to get me out of the group, then maybe she should be the one to get me back in. She asked me how I was doing, and I told her not great, but she knew that. She didn't bring up anything that had happened just told me that I could go back to being friends with them, but only after I hung out with her for an evening. She said some guy was interested in me and wanted to meet me. I said, "why would some guy want to meet me?" What I really meant was, if he heard everything about me then he wouldn't even want to be friends with me, let alone more than friends. I also asked her if this was a lie. Was I going to show up, only to be beaten by a bunch of girls like Gwen was. Rochelle assured me it was legit, but she didn't know why this guy wanted to meet me. Rochelle was dating the guy's friend, maybe this was supposed to be some sort of double date. She asked me again, saying it was going to be fun. I told her that I didn't know, and that I had to ask my parents first.

The more I doubted, the more Rochelle seemed desperate for me to come - I told her I would call her back. I asked my parents, telling them I really wanted to go. I told them I wanted back in the group, to have close friends again. They continued questioning me, which actually got me thinking more. I started thinking back to the 'incidents', how mean Rochelle had been recently... I had a gut feeling that if I went to her place that night, things would not turn out well for me - physical harm seemed like a likelihood. I told my parents I no longer wanted to go to Rochelle's and asked them to tell me I wasn't allowed to go, so I wouldn't have to lie when I told Rochelle. Reluctantly, they agreed so I called Rochelle back.

She was not happy and asked me if my parents and I understood the importance of me going to her house to get back in the group. I told her I understood but that there was nothing I could do about it. I said couldn't we do something another time, during the day. She said that was my only chance, if I didn't come that night then I wouldn't be back in the group. I told her I was sorry and that I hoped she would give me another chance. She told me again that this was my only chance, and we hung up. I cried pretty hard but that feeling of unease was so strong that I couldn't just ignore it.

I don't know if Rochelle had intended for something bad to happen to me that night or if she truly thought we would have a good time, but I felt it was either an ambush or that I might get beat around and raped by this guy who wanted to meet me so badly. Guess I still had a little bit of self-survival in me.

I learned quite a lesson that night and that was to slow down and think, think things through before making a decision when I got a strong feeling in my gut, a feeling almost like a panicky tingle. There were plenty of times when I ignored what my gut was trying to tell me later in my life, but I never ignored it when it felt that strong.

I was hard on myself the next couple of weeks, wondering if I had made the wrong decision by not going to Rochelle's. And I wondered if Jane, the unofficial leader of the group, would give me another chance to be friends again.

I kept thinking that I didn't want to me be anymore. I was tired.

I thought of writing some of my thoughts down to get them out of my head. This is the first time I wrote something completely with my own thoughts and words. I loved eagles and what I thought they represented. They were big and strong and beautiful. I thought they ruled all other birds, and that none would dare challenge them. I even wrote a poem about them back then:

> I wish I were an eagle,
> I wish I could change my colors
> Fly above in the sky

So high, so high

Up there, no one can touch me
No one can reach me
I see all, I know all I am
all

I perch on the tallest trees
Watching over everything
I am alive
And no one can take that from me

Back then, I wished humans could morph into animals like in the movies. How different my life would be if I could do that.

Chapter 26

The Prom

Jane started to say hi to me in the hallways again, giving me hope that we would at least be friendly with each other.

Prom night had arrived, and Quinn was coming to my house to get pictures taken with me before we went. He was so handsome in his black tux with his ocean blue eyes. My prom dress was light pink on the top half and burgundy from the waist down. It was form fitting on top and had off the shoulder sleeves. I wore a crinoline to give the bottom half some poof, nothing crazy but just enough to make it pretty. I left my hair the same as I always did, I wasn't much for putting it up and my curls made doing my hair easy. I tweezed my bangs and let my dark brown curls do their thing. Quinn's parents wouldn't come over to take pictures, no surprise but I actually thought they might for Quinn since it was quite a special night. Mom and dad took several pictures though, and then we were off.

It was a warm and perfectly clear that late June night. I was excited, and of course nervous wondering if any of my bullies would be there. I also looked around for Jesse, I knew he had been banned from going to prom, but he could still show up to see everyone dressed up. Quinn was a bit nervous about Jesse too, he knew Jesse was bad news and Quinn was worried Jesse might want to fight him. Jesse and I hadn't officially broken up, but I figure we had. Anyway, he was nowhere to be seen so I relaxed and so did Quinn.

As we arrived, there were tons of kids outside. They were all dressed up, complimenting each other on dresses and tux's, laughing and having a great time. Jane was outside too, with Rachel, whom I had known since grade 1. She seemed happy to see me and said I looked great. So did she of course, she was dressed in a short black sparkly dress, and she had her hair done up fancy. She had curled her wavy hair and had it in a partial updo with the rest of her blond hair resting on her back. Her curls were perfect.

After saying hi to several other people we knew, Quinn and I went into the school hand-in-hand.

Most of the tables in the cafeteria had been taken out, and the rest of the room was a giant dance floor. A bunch of us danced all night. It was mostly the girls dancing to fast songs though and when the slow songs came on, people grabbed their dates and danced to the best 80's rock band love songs. I loved being in Quinn's arms, and I wished the night would last forever, like freezing this perfect moment in time.

Of course there was no way that was going to happen. The dance lasted about 3 hours. I was sad when it was time to go, and everyone was piling out. Jane was having a party and told Quinn we should stop by. I was wary as usual, so Quinn and I lingered in the school parking lot for a while talking. We kissed and I told him how much I had liked him these past 3 years. He said he liked me a lot too and I asked him why he never asked me to be his girlfriend.

I already knew part of it was because of what James' mom had told all the other moms before junior high school and I know he tried to talk to his parents a few times about me because I had been to his house at least a half dozen times. Quinn hadn't actually had a girlfriend in junior high. Maybe he just wasn't totally ready. He asked me if the rumors were true about Jesse and me, and I told him yes but that I wished he had been my first. I started to tear up then and we hugged and kissed some more.

Quinn asked what I wanted to do now, and he brought up Jane's party. I told him I wasn't sure if I was comfortable going but that we would walk the long way around, until we got to her place before we decided. We talked and held hands the whole time walking to Jane's. Quinn was wary of Jesse and asked if I thought he would be at Jane's. I said I had no idea but that it was possible. Quinn was worried again that Jesse would want to fight him if we went inside together, because then he would see Quinn was my date. I would never be able to forgive myself if Jesse even touched Quinn. I told him I would never let that happen, and that I would die for him.

We arrived at Jane's, standing on the sidewalk on the opposite side of the street from her house. We chatted and asked each other what we wanted to do – we were both nervous. I said I wanted to go in, but I also didn't. I was scared of being yelled at, or taunted by Rochelle, and how that would ruin this perfect evening, I was also scared that Jesse might be there, and I was preoccupied with making sure Quinn was safe, and that he would have a good time.

In the end, I decided it was best for Quinn to go to Jane's party and for me to just go home. My house was literally only a minute or two walk from there. I asked Quinn if I had screwed up our chances of being together by being with Jesse. He said he wasn't sure, and I knew right then and there that we would never truly be. I think what was left of anything hopeful and good died in me at that moment, but I didn't want Quinn to know how much I was affected by what he said so we hugged and kissed again, and I told him I hoped he had a really good time. I walked the rest of the way home sobbing, went straight to my room and took off my dress. That perfect night was over.

Chapter 27

The Pit Party

I heard Jane's party was fun. Jesse had been at her place earlier in the evening, but was gone by the time Quinn got there, so I was very relieved. I heard that people were going to go to a pit party for an end of school celebration, and Jane suggested that I go. I don't know if she was disappointed that I hadn't come to her house after prom or not, but she was still trying and that was nice.

As always, I contemplated whether I should go or not. I was nervous who might be there, and that I might be trapped – in that it was in an open area with nowhere to hide. The only way I could get away, if something happened, was to outrun the bullies – and I could probably do that. It pissed me off that I was always worried about getting in a fight, and I told myself I was a coward. I decided to go, mostly because after Quinn and I fizzled, I didn't really give a fuck anymore.

I knew no one that lived by my junior high school would be at the pit party, they were mostly preps (or preppies, kids whose style of dress looked like they went to expensive prep schools) and the pit party was not really their kind of scene. This was more of the tougher crowd scene, where the English and the French Immersion kids who were friends would come together to hang out.

The location of the pit party was close to my old neighborhood. It was an open area with trails of sand and dirt, with trees surrounding the outside. Jane and I had a mutual friend, Rachel, and I went with her to the pit party, she even suggested spending the night at her place if I wanted. Her friendship with Jane had gotten pretty strong in the last little while and I felt good going to the party with her.

When we arrived, there were quite a few people already there, and a big fire was going in the center of the open area. Some were drinking, others drinking and smoking, and I think there was some pot going around as well. I came upon Jane and her friends. Jane seemed happy to see me, but some of her friends weren't. We chatted for a bit, but someone came by and took Jane's attention. I started to walk away, to see who else was around, when Sally yelled at me and asked what I was doing there. I told her Jane had invited me, but she didn't believe me. She started calling me names and making me feel like dirt. I told Sally to ask Jane if she didn't believe me, so she did. Jane confirmed what I had said, and Sally was pissed. As mentioned, Sally really didn't like me, but I never knew why.

Anyway, Sally wasn't having me hang out with them. It's like I was poison, and she couldn't stand me being there, smiling and trying to have a good time. She told me that despite the fact that Jane invited me, she didn't really like me, and nobody wanted me there. She told me I should just do everyone a favour and off myself. I was super mad at first and thought I had never met such a bitch. She told me to leave, and that she better not see me again that night or I was going to get it. I walked away and started sniffling a bit. I had so many thoughts going through my head - Did Jane really not like me? Did anyone give a shit if I was around or not? I thought about my last hope – Quinn – and that was gone. I was a cheater, a betrayer...no love from friends, family or God (again, if he really existed).

I literally had nothing to live for.

As I walked by myself far away from everyone else, I saw something shining on the ground. I went to pick it up and saw that it was a razor blade. It must have been fate, right? Someone had just told me I should kill myself - me finding that razor blade must have been fate. I picked it up and looked at it for a long time. I wondered if it would hurt, how much pressure I would need to put on it to make it cut my skin. I wondered if anyone would find me, try to stop me….so many thoughts. I also recalled all the shitty things I had done that year, and all the shitty things that had happened to me that year too. And with that I made the first slice.

It was more like a scratch though. I didn't know what I was doing, just leaving a red mark without breaking the skin. I tried again in the same spot, a little harder this time. It stung, and a little drop of blood was starting to form, but nothing really. I decided to try above and below where I had tried the first two times, maybe there were more veins in one of those spots. Of course, the razor blade was dull, who knows how long it had been out there. I tried and I tried but I couldn't make the blade cut through my skin. The last attempt was better, causing the whole line to bead blood, but not enough to flow down my arm.

All of a sudden, I noticed someone was coming towards me, asking me what I was doing there by myself. I said I wasn't doing anything, but he noticed the scratches on my arm. Again, he asked me what I was doing. I had known this guy since I was in Grade two, he was a year younger and a super nice guy. He saw that my other hand was clenched in a fist as I was hiding the razor blade. He asked to see what was in my hand, but I wouldn't show him. He decided to take my hand and started peeling my fingers away so I could no longer hide the razor blade. He asked me why I felt I needed to do that. He didn't get it; he didn't know everything that had happened that year. He said that nothing was worth doing that, no matter how bad it seemed. I told him that no one would give a shit. He said that he would, because he had known me for a long time, and thought I was pretty great. He made me promise not to do it again.

After talking some more, he threw the razor blade away and asked if I was going to be ok.

I told him yes and he hugged me. We had been there quite a while, and a lot of people had gone home. It was pitch dark and I started to walk towards the streets nearby. I was still feeling pretty sad even though what that guy said really had a positive effect on me. I thought again of Quinn and how we were never going to be together, and I started thinking about Jesse too. I figured I might as well be with Jesse rather than be alone, he did make me feel safe when we were closer. I kept on walking, and I couldn't see anyone, but I could hear a few voices off in the distance. I thought one of them was Jesse, so I yelled out his name. I yelled three or four times, which must have distracted me, because then I tripped over a chain link meant to keep vehicles out of the pit. I fell hard, really hard, it was like
I did a flip and fell right on my face. I thought I might lose a tooth, but it never happened, thank God...I felt stupid and decided to walk to Rachel's house to see if she was home.

My wrist, at this point, was sore, puffy and red. She was home and really mad at me. She asked me where the hell I had been and said she had been worried about me. She thought something bad had happened. Well, it did but I didn't tell her that or show her what I had done to myself. I called my parents from her house, to pick me up. Unsurprisingly, I had a restless sleep that night. Only that one guy actually knew what I had tried to do. The next morning, my mom noticed the scratches on my arm and asked me what they were from. I lied, and said they were from thorn bushes, because we had been walking in the woods. I think she actually believed me; she didn't press me for more information.

I made a decision about myself that weekend, I decided that if I was willing to off myself then I should no longer fear getting in a fight. I wouldn't die from a fight, maybe be embarrassed but I just didn't give a fuck anymore.

Chapter 28

The Last Week of Junior High School

The last week of Grade 9 was full of games, silliness, and yearbooks. There wasn't much going on in terms of classes, and the teachers didn't mind if we spent it chatting and writing in each other's yearbooks. Most people just said, 'have a good summer', or 'see you in high school'. Some wrote funny things, like the person who wrote along the edge in the middle where two pages connect, "I'm so happy to be the first one to sign your crack". Man, that one made me laugh right out loud.

I was so happy this chapter of my life was soon going to be over, I just wanted to forget about it and about everyone. There was one person who didn't want me to forget though and I figured I would have to deal with her.

I went home for lunch every day that week and on my way back to school one day, Clarissa was waiting for me. At first, I thought of going back and finding a different way back to the school, but I stopped myself and thought "let's see what happens". I was pissed, and the more I walked towards her the madder I got. I thought of all the times she had made me scared and made me feel like crap.

I decided I was ready for this.

Clarissa was happy she had finally caught me alone, there was only about 5 minutes left of the lunch-hour. Clarissa started yelling at me, saying she wanted to fight me. People started to gather, watching us. Feeling bold, I asked her why, what had I ever done to her. "Nothing" was her answer, which made me even more angry. I said, "You don't even know me, you don't know anything about me, so you have no business wanting to fight me". That made her think for a minute which was kinda cool.

She said, "I don't like you". Raising my voice, I snapped back, "Yeah, join the club".

A couple of the on lookers started to shout "Fight, Fight". Kids did this to egg the potential fighters on to go through with it and start fighting, while drawing more people to watch. Man, some people are dumb. I gave that person a major death glare and said, "There isn't going to be a fight". Clarissa asked why and I said, "I already told you why, you have no reason to want to fight me and I am not going to get kicked out of school for you". I said that in as bitchy a voice as I could muster, because I wanted her to know that I didn't think she was worth it, she wasn't worth my time. I also told her that she didn't know, nor did I know what I could do in a fight. I had never been in one before, but I had a lot to be pissed off about. I told her to go ahead but that I wasn't going to do anything. She seemed to mull my words over for a second and she actually decided to walk away. I was very happy with myself, even though everyone who had gathered was disappointed.

I couldn't believe it and I actually got even more mad. I thought to myself, if all it would have taken for her to back down was for me to show that I wasn't scared of her then I wish I had done it a long time ago. I let her and others have this power over me, I walked around in fear, fear of getting hurt. Well, I got hurt, I got hurt a lot and I truly believe the mental fear and games were way worse than any fight would have actually been, but I let it happen, I never fought back, I never stood up for myself, I let them have control over my life. Never again.

What happened to Karen after that?

High school and university of course.

Chapter 29

What I wished I had known and done differently

1.   It's better to get in a physical fight or two, than to let bullies get in your head and affect your mental well-being. Having bullies in your head means you can never get away from them, no matter where they are. They are whispering in your ear 24/7, making you believe things about yourself that just aren't true.

2.   If you get in a physical fight, and you get a few punches in, your bully will most likely stop bullying you. Bullies like to think you are scared and weak, punch them a few times and they will know you aren't scared anymore. They will no longer have power over you.

3.   Talk to an adult about what is going on before you get dark and start thinking about suicide or seriously injuring your bully(ies). If I had talked to someone, an adult, maybe things would have been better from that very first year. You owe it to yourself to take a stand and improve your life then to sit there a take the shit that someone dishes out to you.

4.   Taking a self-defence class will help teach you how to protect yourself. I wish I had done this; I know, beyond a shadow of a doubt, that I would have been much more confident if I had taken some kind of self-defence class. You may think you don't like violence, but it's not about that. It's about giving yourself power over your own life, giving you some confidence.

5.   Your bully probably has a pretty crappy life. I know there are many types of bullies. Mine weren't the rich jocks, or the popular mean girls. Mine were mostly girls who weren't welloff and had trouble at home. Point is your life will eventually be way

better than theirs's will ever be. You will move forward, they will not.

6.   You will go farther than your bully could ever imagine. You are smarter than them, and eventually you will be out of their reach.

7.   In most cases the bullying will stop in high school or university. – your bully won't be with you in university. I know this isn't always true, but it was in my case. Most of my bullies never went past high school.

8.   Learn to be brave and look confident, even if you don't feel that way inside. I truly believe that my bullying started that time in the locker room. I was surprised and scared that Clarissa got so mad and so I cowered. I gave her strength by not standing up for myself and telling her she was blowing it way out of proportion. I said nothing, just that I wasn't looking at anything in a sheepish way. I 0wish I had yelled at her and stood up for myself right from the start.

9.   Bullies will back down if you show them confidence. If they don't think they can intimidate you, they won't.

10.   Listen to your gut, it is trying to keep you safe. You are made for self-preservation. When your body is trying to tell you that something is off, that something bad is going to happen, you must listen. It could save our life.

11.   Parents, teach your kids from a very young age to love themselves, to be proud of themselves and to find something unique and special they are good at. Kids' parents that aren't present in their children's lives, who don't feed them with love and encouragement, who don't tell them there are people out there who may want to hurt them in some way, are not helping their kids

grow and develop fully. It doesn't help to shield them and make them think life is full of bunnies and rainbows. Tell kids the truth so they can be ready, so they can get the tools they may one day need to help themselves.

With so much strength and love,

The end.

www.ingramcontent.com/pod-product-compliance
Lightning Source LLC
La Vergne TN
LVHW091224080426
835509LV00009B/1161